100 MOTORCYCLES 100 YEARS

THE FIRST CENTURY OF THE MOTORCYCLE

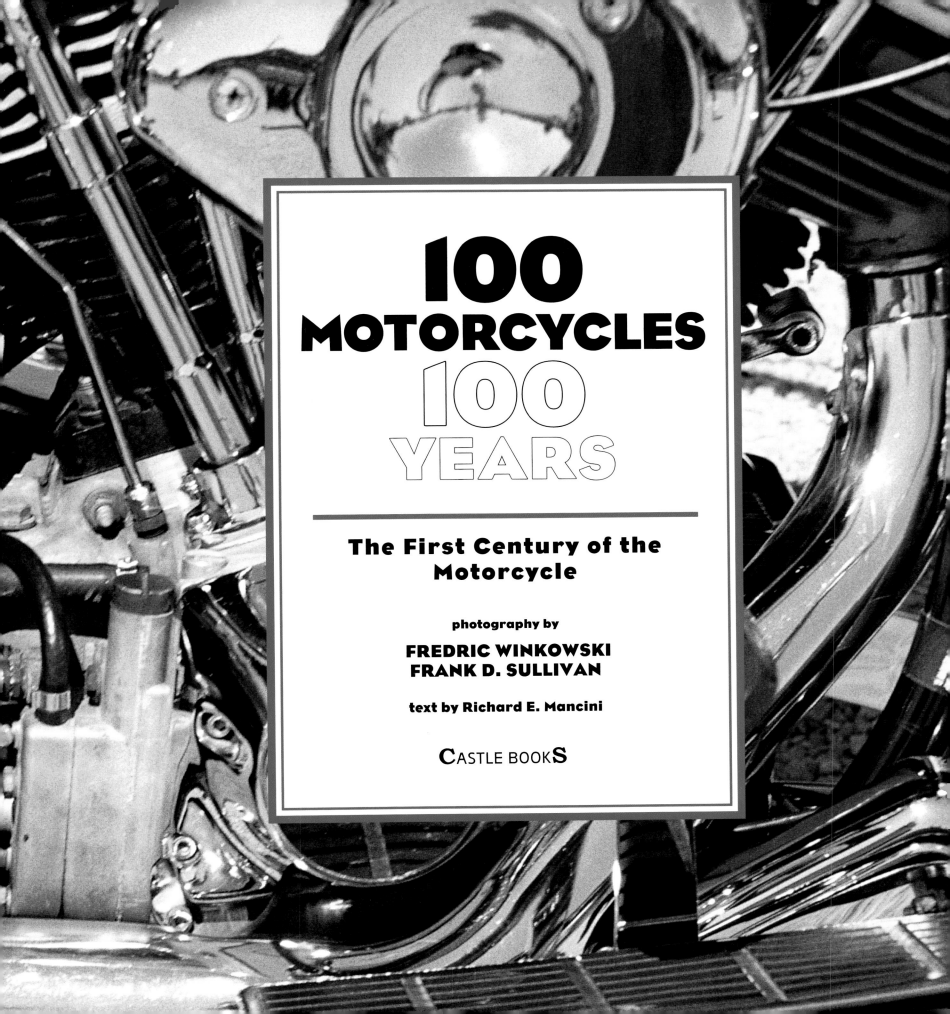

100 MOTORCYCLES 100 YEARS

The First Century of the
Motorcycle

photography by

FREDRIC WINKOWSKI
FRANK D. SULLIVAN

text by Richard E. Mancini

CASTLE BOOKS

This edition published in 2003 by

CASTLE BOOKS ®
A division of Book Sales, Inc.
114 Northfield Avenue
Edison, New Jersey 08837

Published by arrangement with
Frederic Winkowski Photo Publications
48 West 71st Street
New York, New York 10023

1 0 9 8 7 6 5 4 3 2 1

Library of Congress Cataloging-in-Publication Data

Winkowski, Fred.
    100 motorcycles, 100 years : the first century of the motorcycle / by
    Frederic Winkowski, Frank D. Sullivan ; text by Richard E. Mancini.
        p.   cm.
    Includes index.
    1. Motorcycles—History. I. Sullivan, Frank, 1942-   . II. Mancini,
Richard E. III. Title. IV. Title: One hundred motorcycles, one hundred
years.
  TL440.W55   1999   98-48210
  629.227'5'09—dc21   CIP

ISBN: 0-7858-1670-4   Printed in China

C O N T E N T S

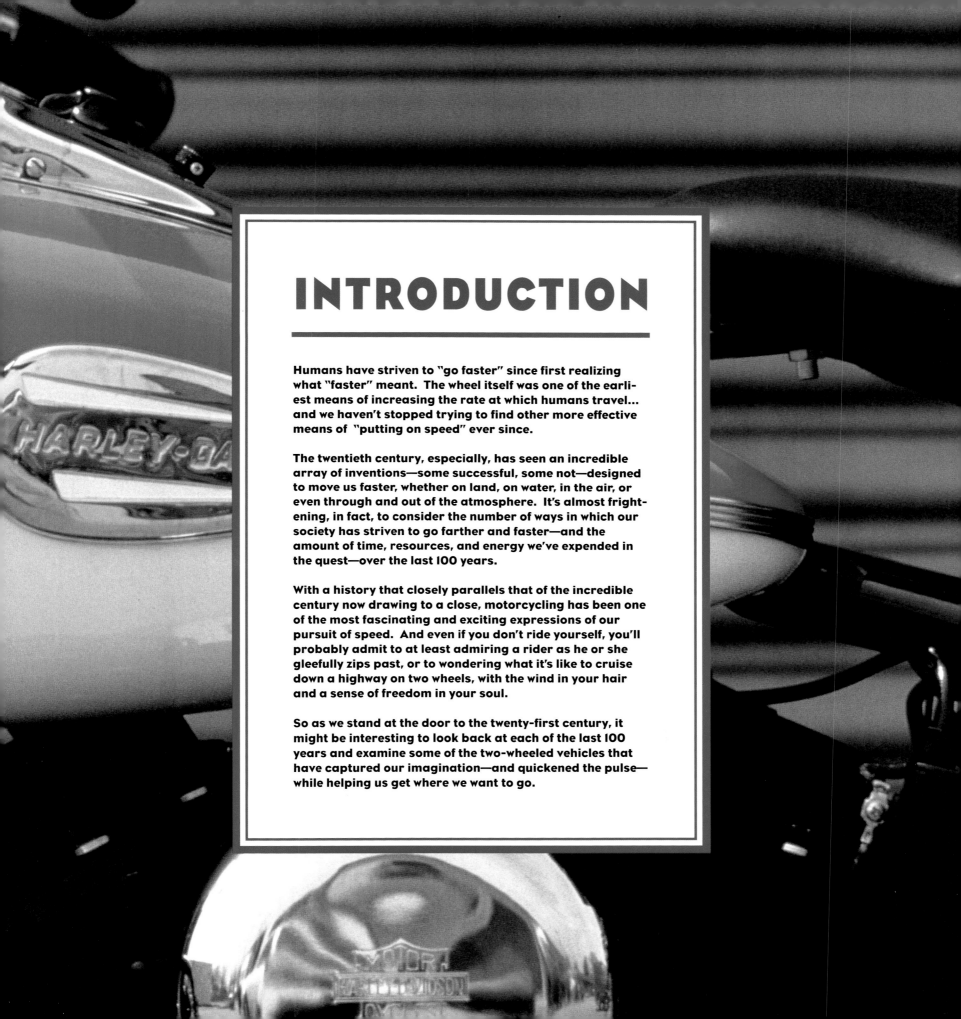

INTRODUCTION

Humans have striven to "go faster" since first realizing what "faster" meant. The wheel itself was one of the earliest means of increasing the rate at which humans travel... and we haven't stopped trying to find other more effective means of "putting on speed" ever since.

The twentieth century, especially, has seen an incredible array of inventions—some successful, some not—designed to move us faster, whether on land, on water, in the air, or even through and out of the atmosphere. It's almost frightening, in fact, to consider the number of ways in which our society has striven to go farther and faster—and the amount of time, resources, and energy we've expended in the quest—over the last 100 years.

With a history that closely parallels that of the incredible century now drawing to a close, motorcycling has been one of the most fascinating and exciting expressions of our pursuit of speed. And even if you don't ride yourself, you'll probably admit to at least admiring a rider as he or she gleefully zips past, or to wondering what it's like to cruise down a highway on two wheels, with the wind in your hair and a sense of freedom in your soul.

So as we stand at the door to the twenty-first century, it might be interesting to look back at each of the last 100 years and examine some of the two-wheeled vehicles that have captured our imagination—and quickened the pulse— while helping us get where we want to go.

The Chronology

The authors have considered each year since 1900 and selected a classic motorcycle, either produced or sold in that year, or otherwise connected with a significant historical event or trend of that year. We based our selections on a number of criteria, including historical importance, uniqueness, aesthetic qualities, technical innovations, significance of a model to its make (or "marque"), availability of an original or restored example, the bike's personal history, and, of course, visual excitement and just plain fun!

We've selected both restored and unrestored machines, most of which are in running condition, but some of which are not. Most of the motorcycles on these pages are privately owned, while a few are part of museum collections or exhibits. Some are ridden everyday, while others are not ridden at all due to the fragility or value of the individual machine.

The Marques

The production of this book has been a process filled with constant discovery, especially concerning the marques of motorcycles, due to the simple fact that more than 3,400 individual marques of motorcycles have been produced and marketed during the twentieth century! In fact, it hasn't been unusual to run across a "new" marque (new to us, at least) on any given day.

Although the 100 motorcycles in this collection represent a wide variety of significant marques from throughout the twentieth century, no attempt has been made to give equal representation to any marque or group of marques, since this would be impossible. We have, however, striven to impart as much information about significant marques and individual models as availability and space would allow.

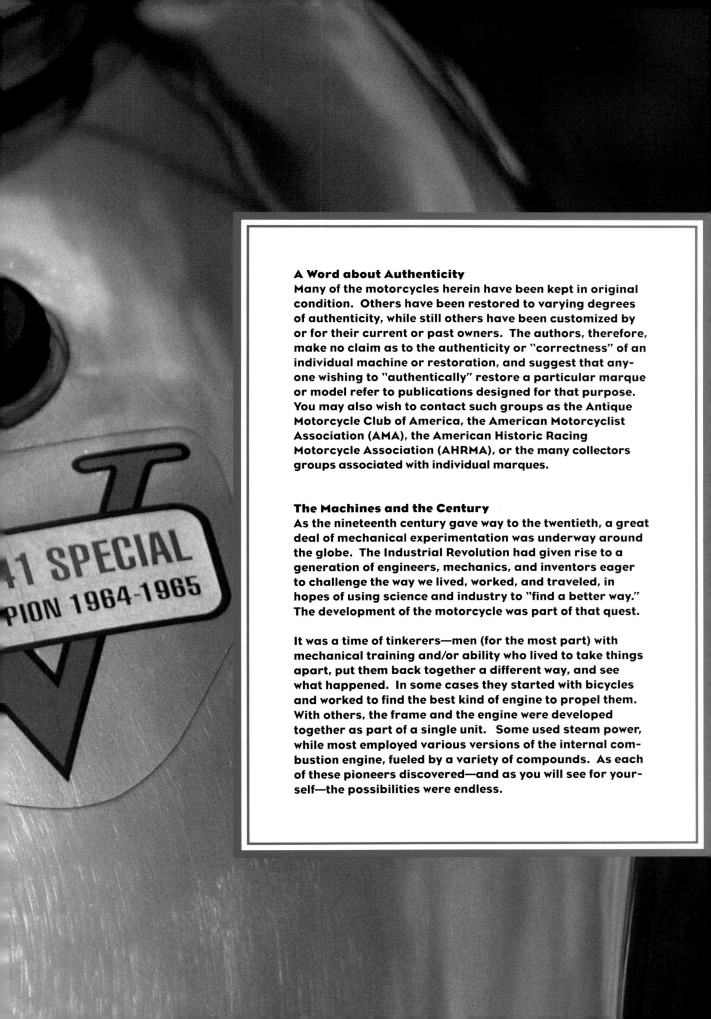

A Word about Authenticity

Many of the motorcycles herein have been kept in original condition. Others have been restored to varying degrees of authenticity, while still others have been customized by or for their current or past owners. The authors, therefore, make no claim as to the authenticity or "correctness" of an individual machine or restoration, and suggest that anyone wishing to "authentically" restore a particular marque or model refer to publications designed for that purpose. You may also wish to contact such groups as the Antique Motorcycle Club of America, the American Motorcyclist Association (AMA), the American Historic Racing Motorcycle Association (AHRMA), or the many collectors groups associated with individual marques.

The Machines and the Century

As the nineteenth century gave way to the twentieth, a great deal of mechanical experimentation was underway around the globe. The Industrial Revolution had given rise to a generation of engineers, mechanics, and inventors eager to challenge the way we lived, worked, and traveled, in hopes of using science and industry to "find a better way." The development of the motorcycle was part of that quest.

It was a time of tinkerers—men (for the most part) with mechanical training and/or ability who lived to take things apart, put them back together a different way, and see what happened. In some cases they started with bicycles and worked to find the best kind of engine to propel them. With others, the frame and the engine were developed together as part of a single unit. Some used steam power, while most employed various versions of the internal combustion engine, fueled by a variety of compounds. As each of these pioneers discovered—and as you will see for yourself—the possibilities were endless.

1900
De Dion-Bouton
Tricycle

In 1899, American millionaire Harold Vanderbilt commissioned French engineer Georges Bouton and financier Count de Dion to produce a machine to pace board-track bicycle races at New York's original Madison Square Garden. Appearing three decades after the first known "motorcycle"—the French Michaux-Perreaux Steam Velocipede of 1868—the motorized tricycle created by the de Dion-Bouton effort was among numerous early attempts at applying gasoline-powered engines to what were still essentially bicycle designs.

Capable of a top speed of 20 mph—quite peppy for its day—de Dion-Bouton's 1-3/4-hp engine enjoyed such success that its design was copied around the world, but unfortunately with little benefit to its inventors. This original 100-year-old late-Victorian machine, first restored in 1939 and again in the 1990s, stands as a shining, if curious, example of state-of-the-art motorcycling at the dawn of the sport's first century.

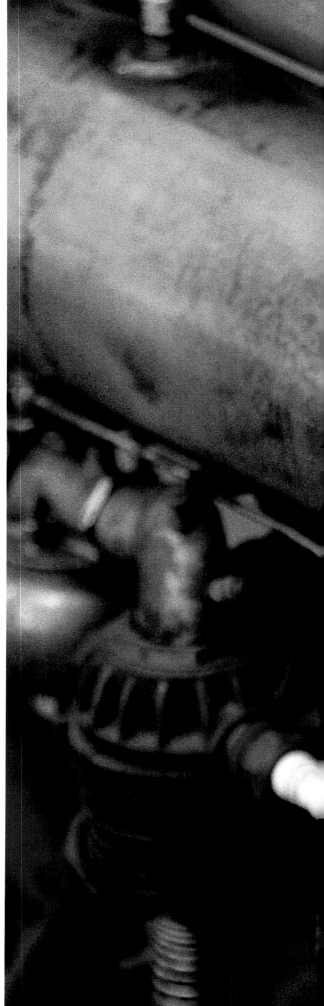

1900-1909

A new century dawns to the sound of the tinkerers and their bicycle engines.... In backyard sheds, pioneers Norton, Harley, Werner, Scott, Davidson, Gilera, and Brough build their first machines. Tourist Trophy racers meet to compete at the Isle of Man. By the decade's end, a new industry is in full swing.

1901
Thomas

Innovative and inspired, the early motorcycle pioneers nonetheless had to work with what turn-of-the-century technology had to offer. That usually meant a bicycle of the day, and their own variations on the internal-combustion engine. This American-made Thomas machine from 1900–1901 is a marvelous example of what those inventive souls could create.

1902
Werner

In Paris, the work of two expatriate Russian brothers, Eugene and Michel Werner, had a profound effect on modern motorcycle design. They built an 1897 machine that placed a De Dion-Bouton engine above the front wheel, driven by a rawhide belt. Though its forward engine position caused handling problems, this early "front-wheel-drive" bike actually produced a smoother ride than De Dion-Bouton's own motorized tricycle.

But in 1901, the Werners forever advanced motorcycle design beyond the "bicycle-and-engine" concept with the machine shown here. Splitting the frame just in front of the pedals, they created a gap between the two down-tubes and placed the 2-hp 230-cc engine into it, thereby improving weight distribution and handling. They also incorporated an improved spray-type carburetor, a vacuum-operated inlet valve, front and rear rim-brakes, and electric ignition—resulting in what is considered one of the first "true" motorcycles.

The new Werner machine, represented here by a 1903 model, not only sold well, but also dominated the international motorcycle races held in 1902.

Actually quite elegant, the Thomas is typical of many "primitive" motorbike designs, employing a single-cylinder 1.8-hp engine adapted to a bicycle frame. From today's viewpoint, this machine's sloping engine placement—in the center of the frame, just above the pedaling gear—looks quite natural. At the time, however, it was just one of several areas in which designers chose to put a motorcycle's power-

plant, others being above the front wheel, behind the seat, or even at the back of the bike.

Built under the auspices of the Thomas motorcar company, this early belt-driven gem could manage a top speed of about 25 mph.

1903
Clement

The year that witnessed the Wright Brothers' flight at Kitty Hawk was also a banner year for the worldwide motorcycle industry. Americans Bill Harley and the Davidson Brothers unveiled their first production motorcycle in 1903, as did Triumph in Great Britain, Belgium's Fabrique Nationale (FN), and Czechoslovakia's Laurin & Klement. And in France, the pioneering automotive firm Clement built this early motorbike featuring the overhead-valve engine it began producing a year earlier.

An interesting variation on the "clip-on"-engined motorized bicycle, the fenderless 1903 Clement seen here sported a 142-cc single-cylinder motor with a large outside flywheel, which drove the rear wheel via a tensioner and leather belt. The bike also featured both front and rear suspension—in front by means of girder forks, and in back through a telescopic down-tube—and a steel fuel tank mounted below the handlebars.

1904
Phoenix

Founded in England in 1900 by former bicycle-racer-turned-motorcyclist J.V. Hooydonk, the Phoenix marque stayed in production through most of the new century's first decade. Like other machines of its day, the Phoenix initially used engines built by Minerva, the Belgian firm that not only produced its own bikes, but also licensed and exported powerplants for use by other cycle makers around the world. Early Phoenix motorcycles employed 211-cc and 345-cc Minervas, while later models featured motors of the company's own production and design.

A machine of excellent design, the Phoenix carried its single-cylinder engine below the forward down-tube, in roughly the same position as is found on the British Excelsior. A fairing behind the rear down-tube was designed to match the fuel tank mounted below the crossbar. This extraordinary example of a 1904 Phoenix is rigged to haul an unusual, two-wheel wicker trailing basket.

1905
Matchless Single

With its supremely confident name and a string of early racing successes, Matchless was among Britain's first and greatest cycle makers. The family-owned firm, headed by H.H. Collier (and later by his sons Harry, Charles, and Bert), began production in 1899 at a factory in Plumstead Road, in the Woolwich section of London.

The marque's fame came early in the new century, when racing brothers Charlie and Harry Collier registered a succession of victories atop the family's Matchless machines, most of which were powered by JAP (J.A. Prestwick) engines. Charlie, in fact, won the very first Tourist Trophy (TT) single-cylinder race on the Isle of Man in 1907, riding a 432-cc over-head-valve bike that was not so far removed from the nicely restored 1905 Matchless single seen here. The following year Charlie placed second, while Harry won in 1909 and then placed second in 1910, when Charlie emerged victorious again.

Matchless took over AJS in 1931 to form Associated Motor Cycles, which remained one of Britain's top manufacturers until the mid-1960s.

1906
NSU

Like its national rival BMW, Germany's NSU was an established manufacturer in another field—first knitting machines, then bicycles, as opposed to BMW's armaments—before engaging in motorcycle production. But Neckarsulm Strickmaschinen Union began building motorbikes in 1901, more than 15 years before BMW entered the field after World War I. The company's earliest bikes were powered by 1.5-hp 234-cc "clip-on" engines manufactured in Switzerland by the French firm Zedel.

Within a few years, however, NSU machines were featuring integrated single-cylinder and V-twin motors of the company's own manufacture, including a water-cooled side-valve single model, which appeared in 1905. Some employed a diagonally positioned engine, while others, such as this restored 1906 3-hp single, placed the motor in an upright position at the center of the frame.

A well-made machine, the early belt-driven "Neckarsulm" (named for the location of the factory) evolved into one of Germany's best-known marques, and, known as the NSU, it enjoyed considerable success right through to the 1960s.

1907
Deronziere

Prior to the Great War, France was a hotbed of motorcycling activity. During the late 1890s, the pioneering teams of De Dion-Bouton and the Brothers Werner both worked and unveiled their first motorcycles there, and French cities hosted some of the first international racing events. After 1900, at least five manufacturers were based in France: Clement, Rochet,

René Gillet, Terrot, and Deronziere, which began producing motorbikes in 1903.

The compact machine featured here is a 1907 Deronziere "Autocycle." Its air-cooled, 282-cc, four-stroke engine produced about 3.5 hp and propelled the bike to a top speed of approximately 20 mph. Innovative features included a sleek fuel tank; a linked drive belt, which drove a pulley connected to the rear wheel by spokes; front suspension via leading-link forks;

and a silencer (the spool-like device just in front of the engine).

Unlike rivals Clement and Rochet, which were gone by 1910, Deronziere survived the first decade of the century—but not by much. The pioneering French firm closed its doors at the outset of World War I.

1908
FN Four

Another longtime European motorcycle manufacturer that started in the arms business, Belgium's FN (Fabrique Nationale d'Arms de Guerre), launched its first motorbike a short time after beginning bicycle production in 1901. The company stayed on the scene for nearly 60 years, but its most influential period came between 1903 and 1924, when it produced the highly innovative machine seen here—the shaft-driven FN Four.

FN designer Paul Kelecom developed this machine's four-cylinder engine and clutchless shaft-drive transmission to combat the engine vibration, belt slippage, and frame fatigue inherent in the single-cylinder designs of the day. The action of the pistons counteracted each other, creating less vibration. And the frame was designed to accommodate the large 498-cc power-plant suspended between split-bottom rails, with exhaust pipes extending below the driveshaft.

Sporting such other advanced features as rear drum brakes, manual oil pump, and front suspension, the FN Four, represented here by a majestic 1908 restoration, continued in production for another 20 years.

1909

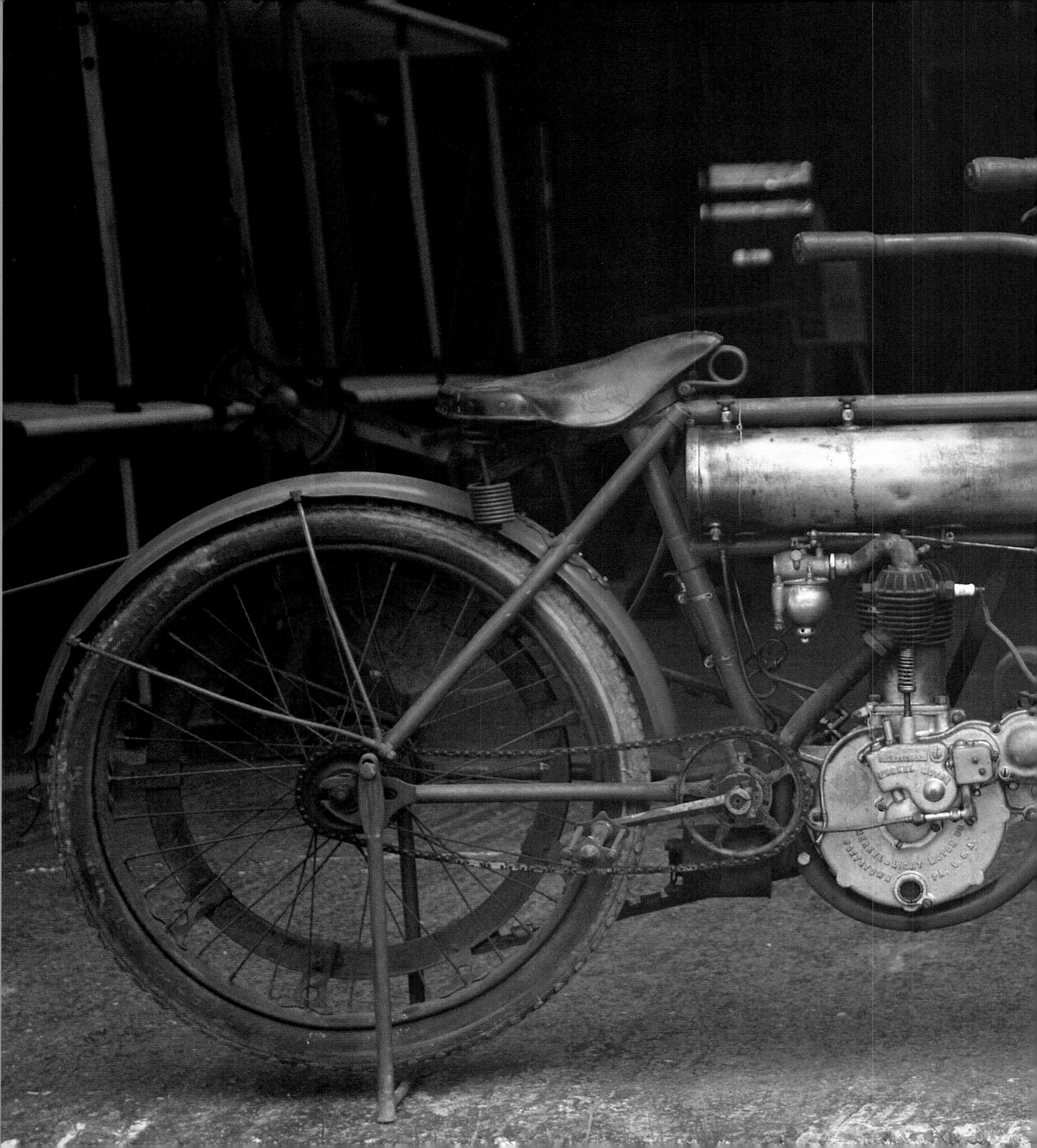

1909
Merkel Light

In the industry since 1902, Merkel produced a series of well-designed single and V-twin motorcycles until the early 1920s. This all-original, blue 1909 Merkel single reflects such common primitive features as atmospheric

intake valves, leather-belt drive, and cylindrical brass crossbar-mounted fuel tank. But the marque employed an unusual segmented drive-belt and influential innovations in its suspension and lubrication systems.

Though chassis suspension was common for the period, the Merkel Light's spring frame allowed the rear wheel to vibrate without altering the drive-train's tension, and sported a forerunner of the telescopic fork. And its unique, throttle-controlled oiling system was literally decades ahead of its time; it would be 20 years before either Harley-Davidson or Indian would adopt a similar method. Although Merkel became yet another victim of the post-World War I decline in the motorcycle market and closed its doors when Indian purchased its Milwaukee plant, this 90-year-old survivor attests to the company's innovative spirit.

1910
Wagner

After ten years of frenetic experimentation and chaos, the motorcycle industry found its way in the second decade of the twentieth century. The year 1910 signaled a boom for two-wheelers around the world. Britain more than doubled its motorcycle export business that year, while registrations of American riders exploded to more than 85,000. And the growing popularity of the annual Tourist Trophy races, begun in 1907, did much to foster enthusiasm for motorcycling as a sport as well as a form of personal transportation.

In the United States, a gaggle of companies entered the bike business, and nearly 30 of them thrived until the onset of World War I. These included Harley-Davidson, Indian, Excelsior, Henderson, Pope, Yale, Orient, Thor, and Wagner, a pioneering firm that produced 1.5-, 2-, and 2.5-hp machines between 1901 and 1914.

This beautiful red 1910 Wagner features a single-cylinder engine mounted into a loop beneath a triangular frame; narrow fenders; natural white rubber tires; and an oil tank beneath the seat. With its chrome handlebars gleaming in the sun, it stands as a shining example of the early American motorcycle.

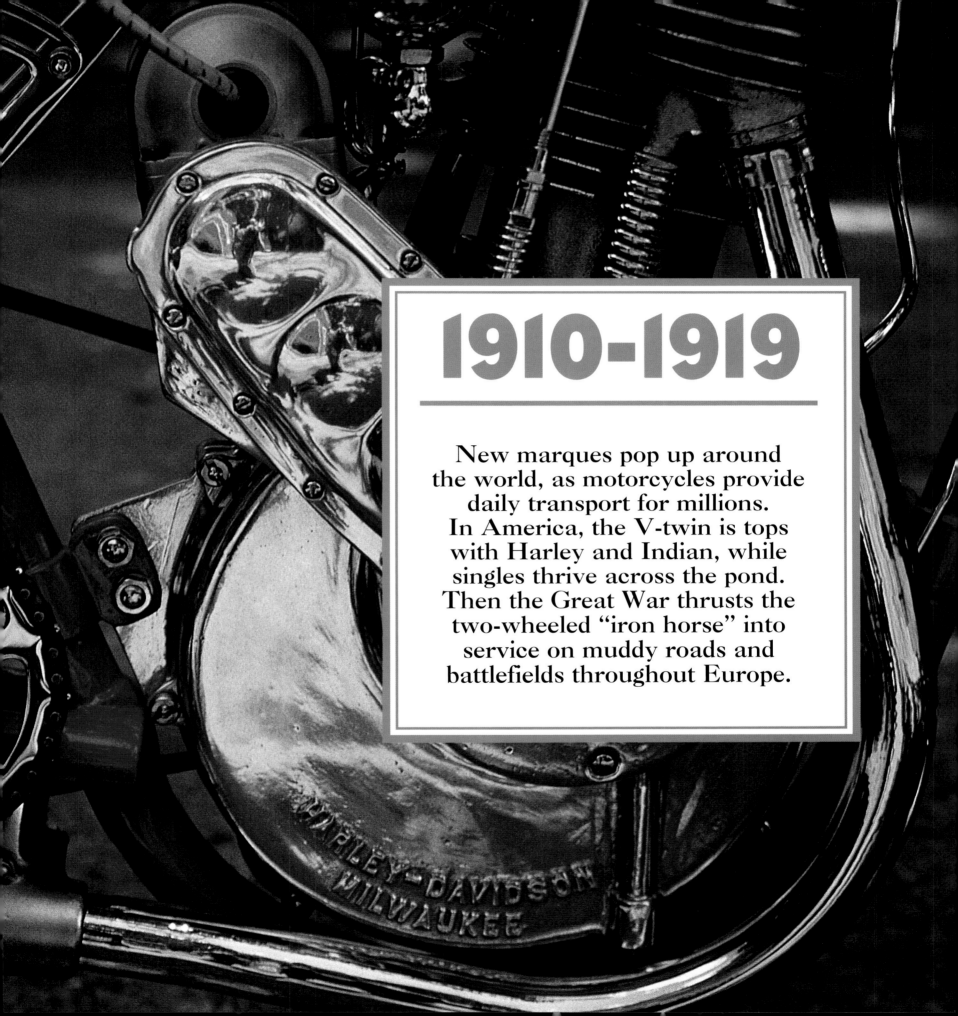

1910-1919

New marques pop up around the world, as motorcycles provide daily transport for millions. In America, the V-twin is tops with Harley and Indian, while singles thrive across the pond. Then the Great War thrusts the two-wheeled "iron horse" into service on muddy roads and battlefields throughout Europe.

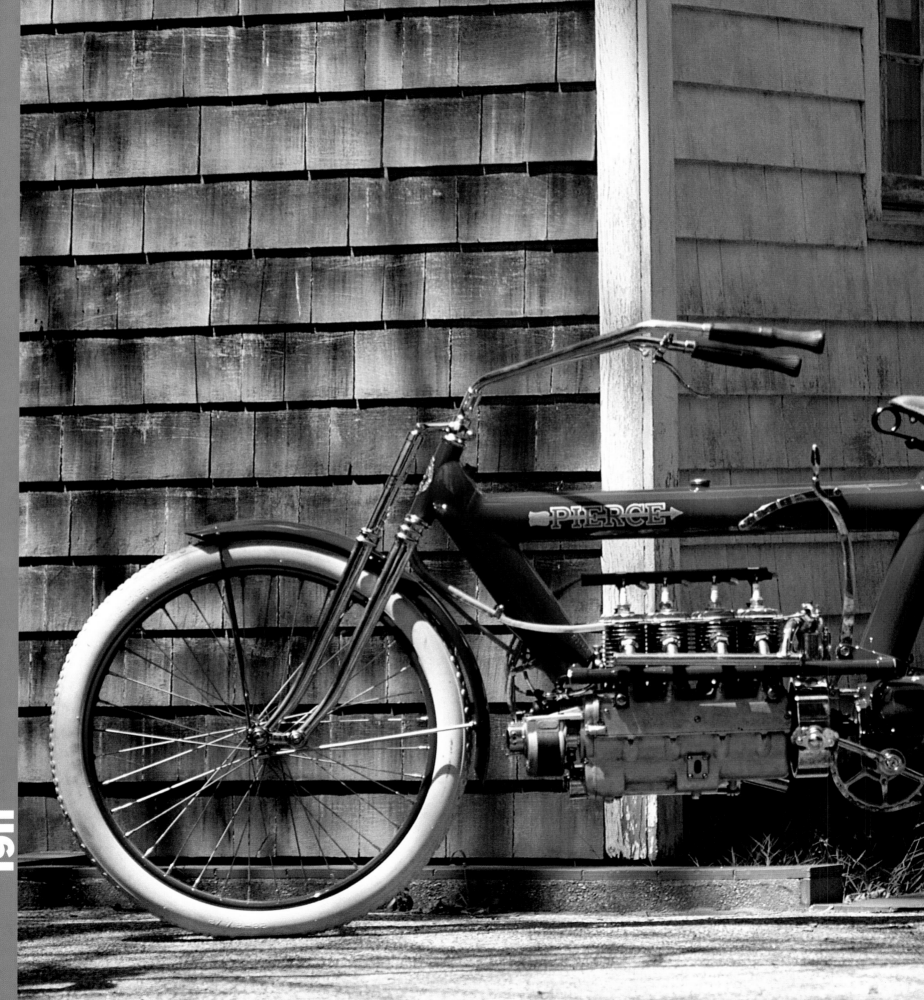

1911
Pierce Four

The parallels between the Pierce Four motorcycle and the Pierce-Arrow luxury automobile were no accident. Founded by Percy Pierce, son of the Pierce Motorcar Company's owner, the Pierce Cycle Company manufactured fine single- and four-cylinder machines starting in 1909.

The first American-built four-cylinder bike, the unique Pierce Four, may have deserved the title "the Rolls Royce of motorcycles." Its in-line, air-cooled, 43-cubic-inch four-cylinder engine topped 60 mph smoothly; its advertising called it "vibrationless" (although the seat was ventilated to prevent injury to the rider's posterior). Featuring an enclosed driveshaft instead of the usual leather belt or chain drive, the innovative design employed a 3-1/2-inch-diameter frame that doubled as gas tank (in the cross-bar) and oil tank (in the down-tube). This expertly restored 1911 machine is one of the few survivors from among the 3,500 made before 1913, when excessive costs put Pierce out of business.

1912 Shaw

Hailing from the American heartland, this machine is a product of the earlier, pre-World War I days of motorcycling in the United States, when many cycle manufacturers were still working their way beyond the bicycle-and-engine concept to "true" motorcycles. Between 1909 and 1923, the Shaw Manufacturing Company of Galesburg, Kansas, produced a series of two models of what were essentially motorized bicycles featuring single-cylinder side-valve engines of their own manufacture, producing either 2-1/2 or 3-1/2 hp.

Driven by the leather belt that other American makers had largely discarded by that time in favor of the chain-drive system still used today, this 1912 model Shaw sports a clutchless 2-1/2-hp single-cylinder powerplant and a gas tank mounted beneath the cross-bar. With its wood-rimmed wheels and delicate looks, this marvelously restored Edwardian-era machine harkens back to a time when motorcycling was still considered something of a gentleman's pursuit.

1913 Harley-Davidson Single

Today, nearly a century after their first experiments with motorized bicycles, their names are virtually synonymous with the American motorcycle. But back when they built their first "factory" prototype—assembled in a backyard shed in 1903—William Harley and Arthur Davidson were just two of cycling's many pioneers.

Although this beautifully restored Harley single dates from 1913—a decade into the marque's history, and two years after its first successful V-twin engine—it features many of the characteristics of the earliest Harley-Davidson machines: a simple, sturdy frame; a single-cylinder engine; a pedal-starting mechanism; a leather-belt drive, and a well-designed, efficient muffler. And, like the rest of the early Harley-Davidson "fleet,"

this octogenarian bike sports the flat-gray paint scheme that inspired the original advertising slogan applied to all of the quiet, dependable Harley-Davidson motorcycles produced prior to World War I: "The Silent Gray Fellow."

1914-1915

1914
Excelsior

As the world tottered on the brink of war in 1914, the American motorcycle industry was thriving. Over thirty makes were in production, and Excelsior was among the leaders. Not to be confused with the British Excelsior marque in production since the late nineteenth century, the "Yankee" Excelsior was manufactured at the Schwinn Bicycle Company's Chicago factory, which in

1917 would also begin turning out Hendersons. In fact, Excelsior would be the only American maker besides Indian and Harley-Davidson to survive the early twenties, and it occupied third place until owner Ignatz Schwinn pulled the plug on motorcycle production in the Depression year of 1931.

Essentially the same bike as the 1914 model, the unrestored 1913 V-twin Excelsior shown here sports a light-gray paint job and carbide headlamp. This machine, still in original but non-running condition, used a leather-belt drive system and was reportedly tough to handle—especially on the none-too-comfortable dirt roads of its day.

1915
Pope

A short-lived, long-vanished American marque, the Pope, was, in its day, the equal of any motorcycle in the world. Longtime bicycle manufacturer Colonel Pope ventured into motorcycle production early in the

century, and by 1911 his company was turning out exceptionally well-designed machines powered by over-head-valve 499-cc singles or 998-cc (61-cubic-inch) V-twins like this 1915 model. A de-pendable motorcycle with plunger-type rear suspension and superb handling, the V-twin Pope pumped out 7 to 8 hp and reached considerable speeds for its time, earning the nickname "Champion of the Hills."

Along with the Cyclone, the Pope was among only a handful of American bikes featuring overhead-valve engines to appear prior to World War I, but it did not survive the industry's wartime decline. In 1918, Pope returned to building the bicycles it had been making since the 1870s. Its final overhead-valve V-twin, in fact, was the last produced in the United States before Harley-Davidson introduced its revolutionary 61E "Knucklehead" in 1936.

1916
Royal Enfield

Royal Enfield was yet another proud British motorcycle firm with a long, storied history stretching from the 1890s to the early 1960s. After producing a "motocyclette" early in the century, then concentrating on parts manufacture for several years, Royal Enfield went back to creating com-

plete machines during World War I. That rich period in Royal Enfield's production is ably represented by the well-ridden 1916 V-twin seen here, which, with its original sidecar, currently entertains air show spectators on the field at New York State's Old Rhinebeck Aerodrome.

Restored from "basket case" condition, the machine is powered by a peppy 750-cc, side-valve V-twin JAP engine, lubricated by a total-loss oiling system, and driven by a unique two-speed "planetary drive" transmission similar to that used in the Model T Ford. Other unusual features include a hand-operated crank-start mechanism located below the seat; unique v-belt rear brakes; and a distinctive sidecar mount, which accommodated a machine gun on its military version.

1917
Indian
Powerplus Twin

Perhaps not as well known as its fabled brothers—the Scout, Chief, and Four—the Indian Powerplus was among that legendary American company's most important models. Introduced in 1916, the 61-cubic-inch Powerplus V-twin engine featured a 42-degree side-valve design that departed radically from the F-head configuration of earlier Indians.

One look at this particular 1917 Powerplus—a roughhewn, unrestored hunk of machine that is still ridden regularly over the rugged landing field of Old Rhinebeck Aerodrome— evokes the very essence of the indestructible Indian.

Although its swing-arm rear suspension provided a relatively comfortable ride for its day, this two-speed, total-loss-oiled Powerplus was and still is an adventure to ride, thanks to such inimitable Indian touches as the "suicide"

clutch (located on the left pedal), the left-hand throttle control, running-board footrests, and "pull-back" handlebars that encourage a straight-up seat position. All in all, it's an original well-worn Indian classic in all its rawboned glory.

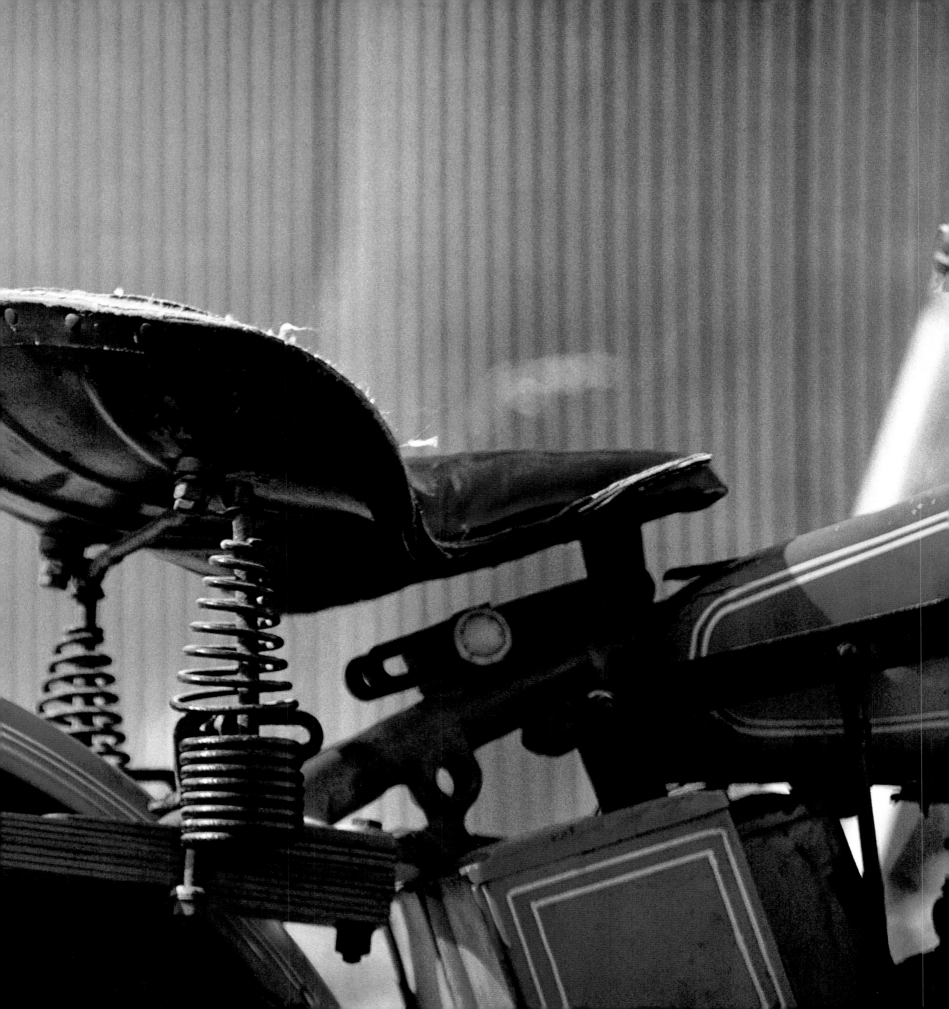

1918
Tusroke

In the last year of the Great War, nearly every motorcycle company across the globe was engaged in producing machines for the armed forces. The new "iron horse" was now a common sight on the battlefields and roads of the war-torn world; a famous photograph of Allied forces entering Germany on Armistice Day shows the first American crossing the border on a Harley. Most combatant nations boasted at least one renowned marque —Germany used NSU, Ardie, and (after occupying Belgium) FN machines; France had Rene Gillet; and American troops rode Harley-Davidsons and Indians. British forces used bikes by Triumph, Douglas,

Clyno, and P & M. Furthermore, despite the conflict, over 150,000 motorcycles were in use by civilians in Great Britain.

Built in Luton, in Bedfordshire, the Tusroke was among the many motorcycles ridden by British citizenry after the Armistice. Powered by a 350-cc two-stroke engine also produced for use in portable generator sets, this restored machine was built in 1918 and sold the following year.

1919
Wooler

A brilliant designer with a taste for the unconventional, Englishman John Wooler spent a long career creating strikingly different motorcycles like the flat-twin model shown here. His first machine, a 344-cc two-stroke built in 1911, was quite advanced for the period, both in frame and power-plant design. The engine employed a flat single cylinder and a double-ended piston, which provided pre-compression within the crankcase, while the frame featured plunger suspension for both the front and rear wheels. Later Wooler motorcycles placed 346-cc and 496-cc flat-twin engines into the same basic frame as the earlier models.

This Wooler, designed and built in 1919, is a 1920 side-valve flat-twin model. A sleek, low-slung chain-driven machine, its styling is rather stunning for its time and includes a distinctive bullet-shaped fuel tank; wide, sweeping fenders; a vivid black-and-yellow paint scheme; and brass accents throughout—including head-lamp, horn, and various engine fittings. Very few machines of that or any era had as compelling a look as the Wooler marque, which remained in production until 1955.

1920
Harley-Davidson
Model J

Harley-Davidson was one of the few American motorcycle companies to survive the "bust" of the early 1920s—brought on by the rise of Ford's Model T—which put most U.S. makers out of business. Moving into the "Jazz Age," Harley competed with Indian for the lion's share of the American market, leaving the others in the dust by developing increasingly better versions of its two-cylinder, 45-degree V-twin engine.

So it was with the Harley-Davidson Model J. The mint restoration of a 1920 Model J shown here illustrates Harley's first use of this 61-cubic-inch (1000-cc) V-twin engine design. A powerful bike for its time, it was capable of speeds approaching 60 mph. Only a limited number of 1920 Model J's were produced, and few have survived the decades. Painted in H-D's standard olive-green color scheme for the U.S. market, this road-worthy vintage example features such extras as a horn, speedometer, and lights.

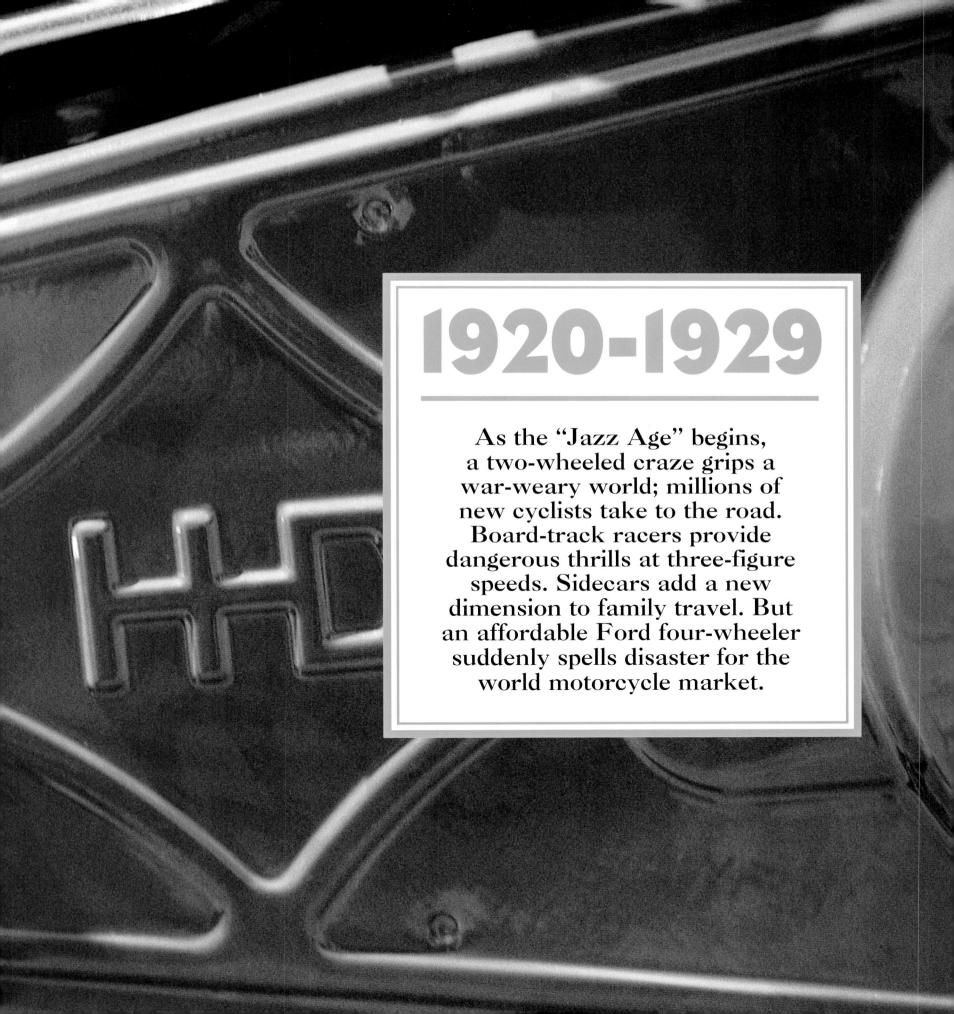

1920-1929

As the "Jazz Age" begins, a two-wheeled craze grips a war-weary world; millions of new cyclists take to the road. Board-track racers provide dangerous thrills at three-figure speeds. Sidecars add a new dimension to family travel. But an affordable Ford four-wheeler suddenly spells disaster for the world motorcycle market.

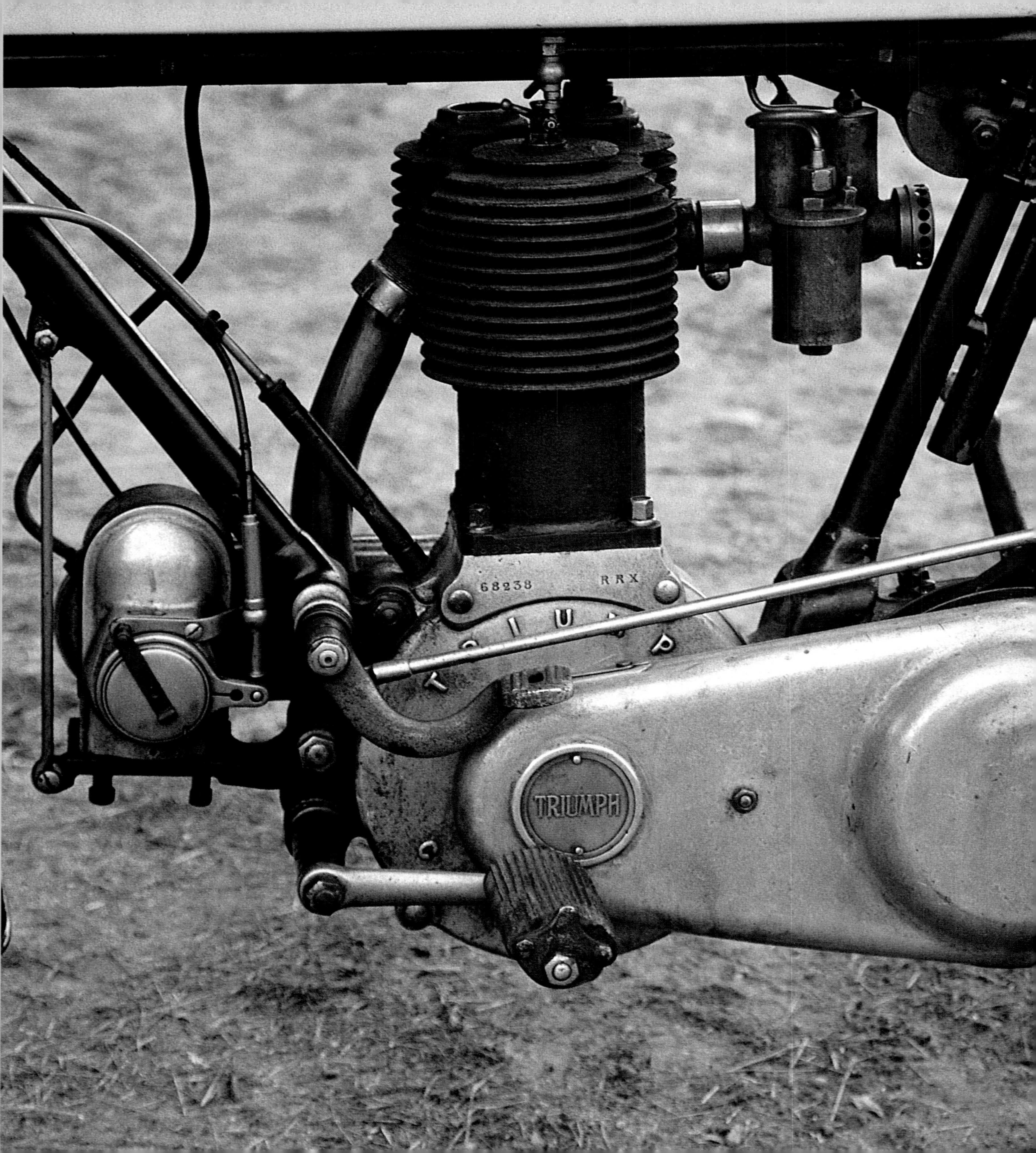

1921

1921
Triumph Single

Long before coming to worldwide prominence in the post-World War II period—largely on the popularity of the parallel-twin engine it had pioneered in 1938—Triumph had been making single-cylinder motorcycles for the British market. Like America's Harley-Davidson, the company had been in business since 1903, turning out singles like this unrestored but complete 1921 model.

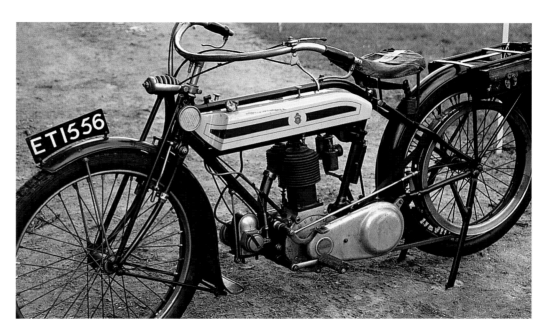

Primitive but fascinating, this belt-driven Triumph is original right down to its license plates. And it can move, too! Propelled to around 70 mph by a 550-cc side-valve powerplant, it employs a total-loss oiling system wherein the lubricant—malodorous castor oil— is burned and expelled. Air and fuel are hand-mixed via a two-chambered carburetor. Although this particular bike appeared in peacetime, it is essentially a war machine; nearly 20,000, with sidecars, were produced for British dispatch riders in World War I.

1922
Neracar

Among the oddest vehicles ever produced, and true to its name, the Neracar was more nearly a car than a motorcycle. Its moniker is actually derived more from the surname of designer Carl A. Neracher, however, than from the fact that this unique "bike," produced in Syracuse, New York, between 1922 and 1925, resembles a two-wheeled car. Like an automobile's, the Neracar's 200-cc engine includes a kingpin, drag link, pitman arm, and tie rod. And its low-slung construction lets it handle like a car; the owner's manual refers to the vehicle's "steering wheel," not "handlebars."

Entirely original, except for its basket, this unrestored Neracar—which languished in a Pennsylvania barn for decades—is kept in riding condition by its owner, collector-racer Doc Batsleer. It's a joy to watch him putter around on this curious relic, whose wide fenders remind us of the days when protecting the rider from horse manure was still a priority.

1923
Indian Scout

As the American motorcycle approached its quarter-century mark in the mid-1920s, one prominent make continued to vie with Harley-Davidson for control of the nation's roads, as it had since the early days—the Indian.

Launched around the turn of the century by Brooklyn-based Swedish machinist Carl Oscar Hedstrom and former racer George Hendee, by the twenties Indian was turning out sleek, stylish machines like this lovingly restored, cherry red 1923 Scout.

This well-crafted Jazz Age beauty sports such period details as the powerful nickel-plated V-twin engine, a tubular-steel frame, trademark rhomboid gas tank, brass acetylene headlamp and tank, white tires (standard issue for their day), frame-mounted controls, leather-covered cables, and classic klaxon horn. More than 75 years after its debut, it remains a sight to see, cruising the open road in the free-wheeling spirit of the "Roaring Twenties."

1924

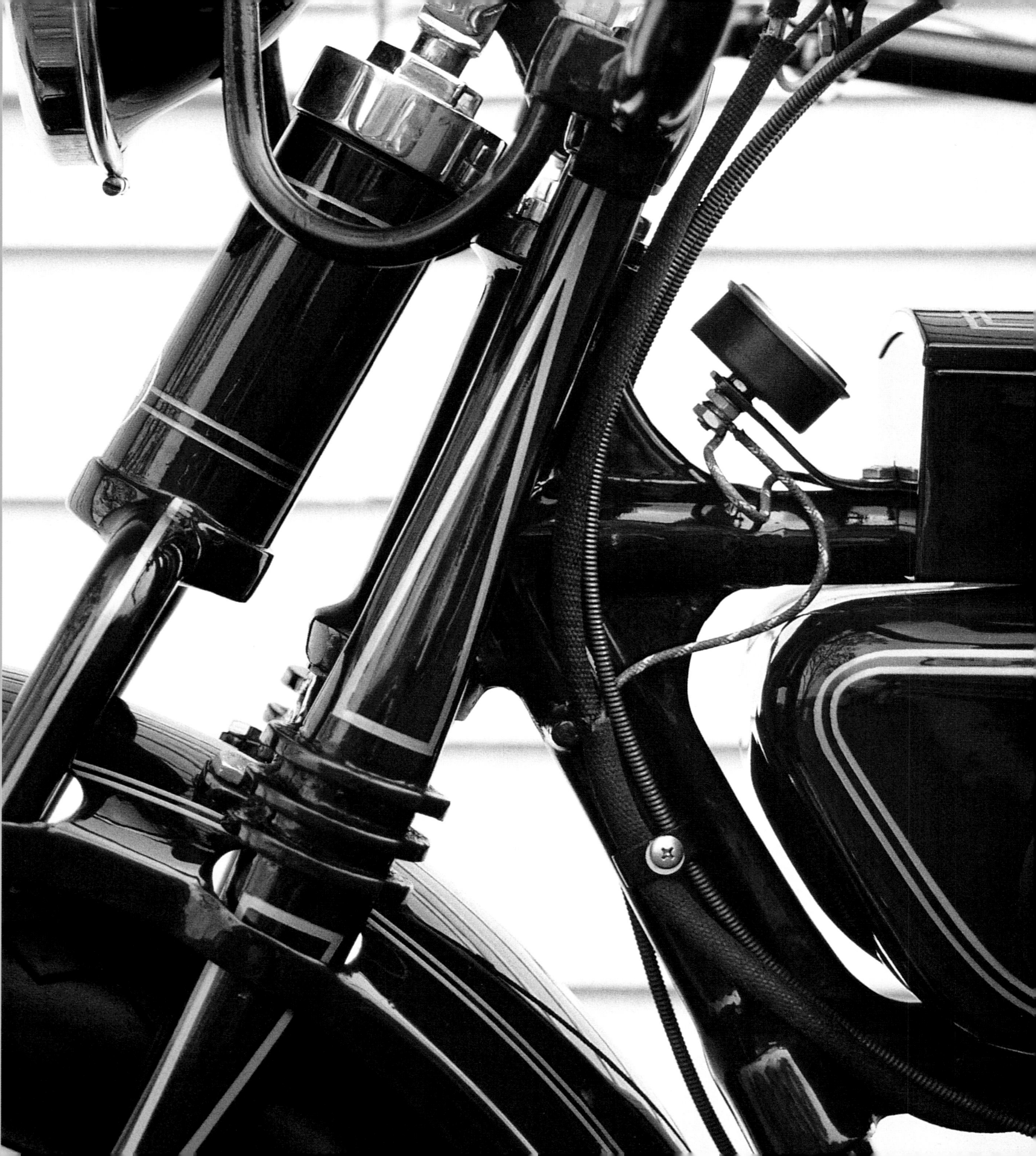

1924
Deluxe
Henderson K

The fact that the Deluxe Henderson K was a kindred spirit to the other preeminent American four-cylinder wonders of the twenties was no accident. Tom and William Henderson, the brothers who first manufactured this extraordinary machine under their own name in the teens, moved on in 1919 to form Ace, which by 1927 had become part of Indian. So both the Ace Four and the Indian Four are cousins of this muscular bike, built after 1917 by Excelsior and thought by many to be deserving of the nickname "the Rolls Royce of motorcycles."

Powered by an air-cooled, 65-cubic-inch side-valve engine, the 1924 K seen here featured state-of-the-art technology for its day: electric lighting, wet sump lubrication, a clutch, two-speed transmission, and manual starting. Its in-line engine arrangement set the standard for American Fours until the early 1940s, when the success of Harley-Davidson's V-twin put an end to U.S. four-cylinder production altogether.

1925
Harley-Davidson
Model JD

After the road dust kicked up by the revolutionary success of Henry Ford's Model T in the early twenties had settled, only the "Big Three" American cycle makers emerged unscathed. The middle of that tumultuous decade saw Harley-Davidson entrenched as number two behind Indian and ahead of Excelsior/Henderson. While the engineering of its 74-cubic-inch V-twin improved, the "Silent Gray Fellow," although now sporting the olive-green paint scheme it had picked up during World War I, was looking a little tired.

The styling exemplified by this side-car-equipped 1924 Model JD, complete with quasi-military "artillery"-style wheels and Army-inspired color, would be obsolete by the time the bike was purchased in 1925. So would the loop frame, square gas tank, and other "antiquated" features that had epitomized Harley-Davidson machines for the first quarter of the century. The model year 1925 welcomed a new look for Harley-Davidson, and the marque's styling finally began to catch up with its technical advances.

1926
Harley-Davidson
Racer

Ironically, America's best-known motorcycle got off to a slow start as far as racing is concerned. Competition was not high on Harley-Davidson's agenda; the first Harley single "racer" was ridden by Walter Davidson in 1909, a decade into the motor company's existence. But Walter's victory in that Long Island Reliability Run—and the publicity it generated— illustrated the value of competition to company brass, and Harley-Davidson racing bikes were here to stay.

Over the next decades, Harley's racing teams garnered victories in such important national meets as the annual 300-mile Independence Day race at Dodge City, Kansas. After winning the 1915 event, Harley-Davidson developed a competition eight-valve overhead-valve V-twin. A Harley with the new engine captured the 1916 Dodge City race and set the standard for generations of Harley-Davidson competition bikes. By the time the 1926 machine seen here appeared, Harley-Davidson machines had become the first racers to top 100 mph—and their descendants still dazzle the competition more than 70 years later.

1927
Indian Flat-Track
Racer

Competition was always an important part of Indian's program, and the marque enjoyed great success in various racing venues—from early board track to dirt track, speedway, and hill-climbing—until the company's demise in the early fifties. During Indian's racing heyday, riders usually rode for the company itself or for dealers who received promotional machines, so few Indian "race jobs" were actually sold.

In fact, the tag of the Brooklyn dealer who originally owned this unrestored 1927 Indian flat-track racer is still on the gas tank today!

Original except for its tires (replaced several years ago) and spark-plug wires, this single-cylinder cycle was designed to race (without brakes) on a flat dirt track, and it featured sprockets for mile and half-mile runs.

Rescued from a Brooklyn basement in the 1970s and actually raced since then, it's as pure and rawboned as any vintage Indian racer one could hope to find.

1928
Harley-Davidson
Model JDH

As the 1920s progressed, so did Harley-Davidson's V-twin engine designs. The company followed the 61-cubic-inch V-twin engine from its 1920 Model J with a bigger 74-cubic-inch powerplant in 1921. But while the Harley's engines steadily improved, its "looks"—dominated by a high frame and boxy gas tanks—remained rather stodgy.

The marque's styling, however, leaped forward in 1925, with a redesign of the frame and fenders, and the introduction of a streamlined tear-drop tank. Gone was the outdated look of the "Silent Gray Fellow," and in its place was "the shape of things to come."

On the sharp-looking 1928 Harleys, buyers could choose between a 61-cubic-inch V-twin "F-head" in the JH, or the 74-cubic-inch version in the JDH seen here, with its top mark of 90 mph. But within two years the F-head would be dead, and Harley-Davidson would debut yet another new design—the VL.

1929
Scott Squirrel
Sprint Special

With an alliterative name as difficult to say as its two-stroke engine was to cool, the Scott Squirrel Sprint Special descended from a line of racers that enjoyed great success in the fabled TT (Tourist Trophy) event. This unconventional machine employed a liquid-cooled, 180-degree-firing two-stroke twin engine nearly 30 years after inventor Alfred Angus Scott developed its prototype in 1898.

Since a two-stroke motor fires at twice the rate of a conventional four-stroke engine—and is subject to twice as much heat—it requires more cooling than the typical air-cooled configuration can provide. Scott's design

solved this problem by cooling the twin cylinders, in sealed casings, with water from a radiator mounted within the frame.

Following TT victories in 1912 and 1913, two-stroke Scotts continued to race successfully until competition from four-stroke opponents grew too strong. This unique 620-cc 1929 machine was originally ridden by racer George Silk at 498 cc.

1930
Indian Four
Custom

"Custom" isn't adequate to describe this visionary rebuild of Indian's famous Four. First appearing in 1927 as a rehash of the Ace in-line 1265-cc Four, the Indian Four's performance problems in relation to the Harley-Davidson, as well as its high costs, led to its demise after 1943, and contributed to Indian's overall failure a decade later. But this particular machine by restorer "Wild Bill" Eggers takes the Four to another dimension.

With over 25 meticulous restorations under his belt, Eggers is known for his commitment to craftsmanship. But the rusted hulk of this 1930 Four was so far gone, it was reportedly rejected by a World War II scrap drive. So

Bill set about crafting the ultimate period custom bike, enhancing the original 1930 Indian with elements driven by his imagination and created by his own hands. The magnificent result shown here, displacing 78 cubic inches and aptly dubbed "Renegade," sports a number of unique features, among them a nickel-plated engine, colorful textured cables, and creative decorative work. Feast your eyes, and enjoy this masterpiece.

1930-1939

With belts tightened by the Depression, two-wheeled travel becomes an alternative once again. Despite the lean times, remarkable machines emerge or improve—the Speed Twin, the 61E, the Square Four, the SS100, the Sport Scout. And an even bigger world conflict begins, sending the motorcycle back into the trenches again.

1930

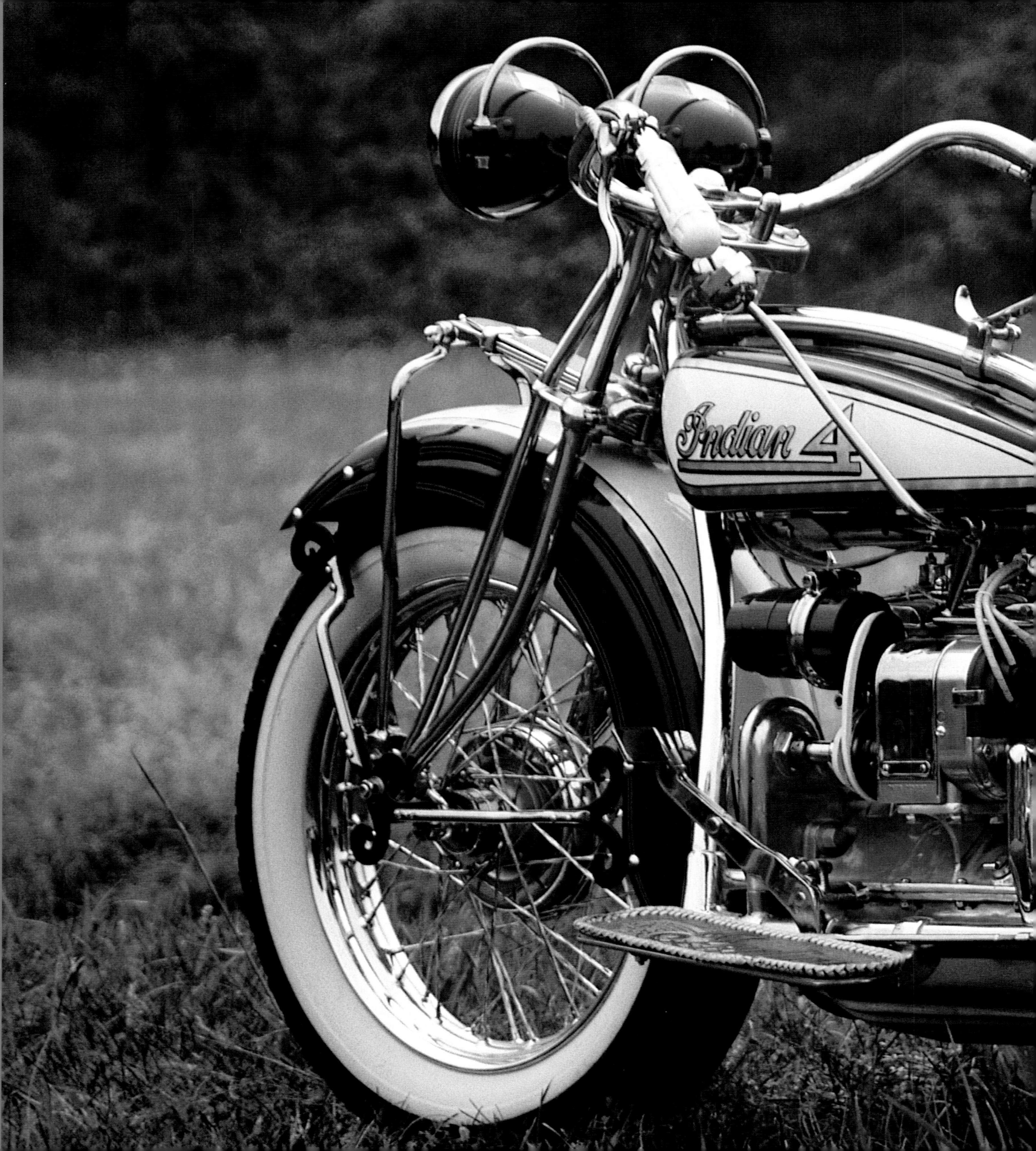

1931
Matchless
Silver Hawk

The year 1931 saw the London-based Matchless company take over struggling AJS, creating the AMC (Associated Motor Cycles) conglomerate. But perhaps more important for the Matchless marque, it was the second year of the Silver Hawk.

Utilizing the same frame as the Arrow, the Silver Hawk featured a powerful element intended to make it a viable luxury alternative to the Ariel Square Four—a 592-cc, overhead-cam V-4. With a powerplant that was essentially two V-twins in one block, the Silver Hawk had a top speed of 80 mph. Its advanced cantilever rear-suspension made it the world's only rear-sprung four-cylinder bike. But although many machines identical to this beautiful 1930 example were sold in 1931, the Hawk couldn't keep up with the Ariel and was discontinued in 1935.

1932
BSA M33II

Names can often be deceiving, as with Britain's Birmingham Small Arms Company. The firm began life in 1863 as an armaments manufacturer. But it was motorcycles—not munitions—that made the name "BSA" famous around the globe.

BSA branched out into the manufacture of bicycles in the 1880s, and by the turn of the century the company was producing quality motorcycle parts for companies in Britain and other nations. But with its first complete motorcycle in 1905, BSA began a tradition that would see it become, for a time, the largest cycle maker in the world.

Built on the success of its fine singles, BSA's reputation was secured on the strength of the bikes it introduced in the late twenties and thirties. These included the popular single-cylinder S27 "Sloper" of 1927 and the reliable M33. Powered by a 600-cc engine, the fine 1933-vintage M33II shown here first hit the market in 1932. With other superb BSA's of the 1930s, it would help the Birmingham firm capture a lion's share of the world motorcycle market over the next several decades.

1933
Harley-Davidson
Model WF

For Americans, one of the most enduring images connected with the motorcycle is that of a police officer atop a muscular bike, pursuing a fleeing perpetrator or pulling over a lead-footed motorist. Perhaps the most recognizable example of a bike at work, the police motorcycle—and the "cop" who rides it—has been a cultural icon throughout the century. And the marque most associated with law enforcement in the United States is—you guessed it—Harley-Davidson. By virtue of the various tasks it has to perform, a police bike must be as maneuverable as it is fast. In the 1930s, Harley's WF machines fit the bill perfectly. With its powerful V-twin, the WF produced all the speed it needed, yet was light enough to handle easily and still carry all the necessary extras. And as this restored silver sheriff's bike (built and originally sold in 1933) shows, there were plenty of extras: regulation siren, red lights, and radio receiver; a baffle to prevent exhaust sparks from igniting road brush; a second speedometer for clocking speeders; and even a notepad for writing tickets!

1934
Ariel VG500 Deluxe

To the uninitiated, the Ariel sounds like "a French motorcycle." But those who know this classic British marque generally love it, whether their machine of choice is the Square Four or the great single models. Beginning life as a bicycle manufacturer, Ariel moved into motorcycle production around the turn of the century, utilizing French engines with tricycle frames. By the 1930s, the company had built a reputation for low, lean, graceful motorcycles, as epitomized by this incredible restoration of a 1934 VG500 Deluxe.

It took a full year to transform this machine from a rust-covered, barn-stored "basket case" to a concours-class show bike. Working from a complete original, restorers gradually brought the VG500 back to life—and the single-cylinder powerplant, chromed twin fishtail exhausts, deeply valanced fenders, and chrome-paneled gas tank gleam as brightly as on the day they left the factory. And it was well worth the sixty-year wait.

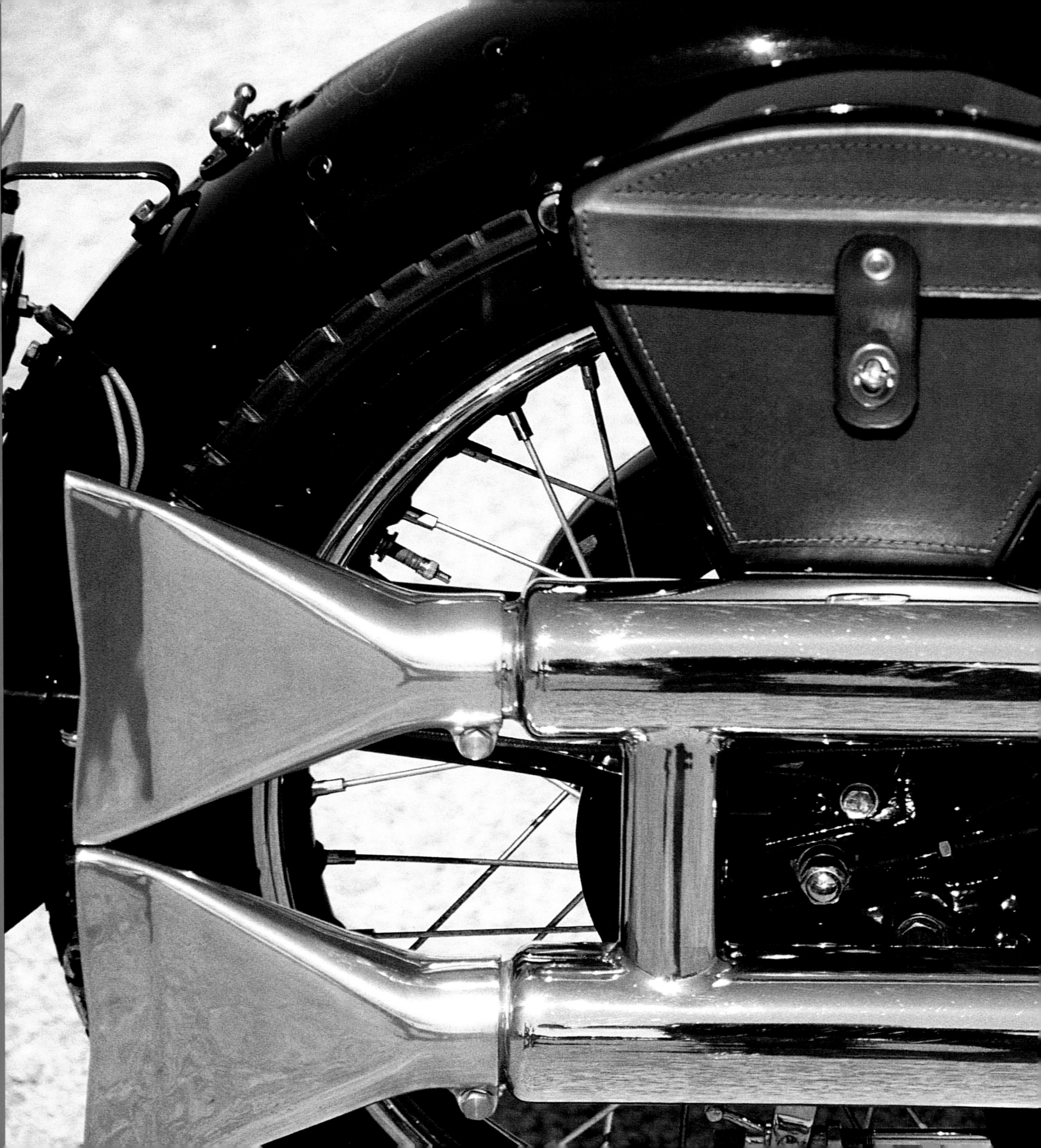

1937
Indian Bonneville
Sport Scout Racer

During the worldwide motorcycle "boom" of the teens and twenties, when Hendee Manufacturing Company's Springfield plant was the largest in the world, Indians had plenty of competition from other U.S. companies. But by the mid-1930s, Indians and Harley-Davidsons were the only American bikes still in production, and they fought head-to-head on the nation's racetracks as well as on its roads. The V-twin Indian Scout, designed by Charles B. Franklin, enjoyed great success from its debut in the 1920s and earned a

reputation for durability: "You can't wear out an Indian Scout." Racing versions—like the 1937 Bonneville Sport Scout Racer shown here—excelled for decades, and they continue to compete in vintage races across America. Originally ridden by midwestern racer Pat McHenry, this venerable machine is now raced under American Historical Racing Motorcycle Association rules by current owner Doc Batsleer, and it has taken a first place at Daytona!

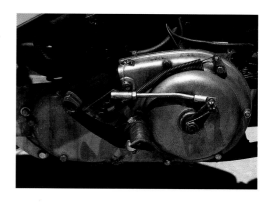

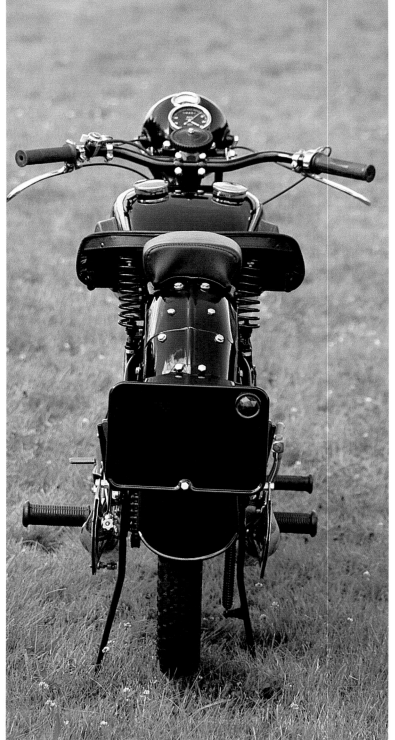

1938 Velocette GTP

One of perhaps only a half-dozen of its kind still on the road in the United States, this majestic machine is typical of the high-quality single-cylinder-engine bikes produced by the British motorcycle industry during the years just prior to World War II. Velocette had been known for sporting singles since its creation in 1905, although the GTP was essentially a commuter bike, providing everyday transportation with a flair.

Styled by former TT rider Harold Willis, Velocette's chief designer in the 1920s and 1930s, the GTP featured a two-stroke single with an outside flywheel and the aircraft-styled hydraulic suspension dampers that Willis initiated in 1936. Velocette had difficulty keeping up with postwar market changes and finally succumbed in 1971, the last of the independent British producers. But its superior bikes, like this 1938 gem restored by Dave Carr, are still going strong after decades on the road.

1939
Harley-Davidson
Model ULH

In late 1939, on the eve of World War II, Harley-Davidson introduced yet another version of the 80-cubic-inch "flathead" V-twin it had previously used (through 1936) in the VLH model. Designated the ULH, this powerful machine was produced by the company's Milwaukee factory during the prewar years of 1939 and 1940 only. Thereafter the company produced the smaller but more efficient "knucklehead" engine that would help Harley-Davidson achieve dominance over Indian after the war.

After purchasing it in complete and original condition, the current owner of the black 1939 ULH seen here had it restored to its former glory. As he remarked while positioning it for these photographs, it's a heavy bike—weighing in at over 700 pounds. But its flathead powerplant can propel the massive ULH to a top end of approximately 85 mph—a commendable speed for its day, and one at which even riders of today's sophisticated Harleys could cruise comfortably.

OVERLEAF

Kicking up dust at every turn, racers from AHRMA (American Historic Racing Motorcycle Association) roar at top speed across a dirt-track course on authentic motorcycles ranging from a quarter- to a half-century old.

1940-1949

Two-wheeled warriors distinguish themselves on every front, in every theater of operation, as war engulfs the globe. Out of the ashes of that conflict come new machines, new markets—and new competition from once-vanquished nations. And a man in a bathing suit rides a motorcycle faster than anyone has before.

1940

HARLE
DAVI

1940 Harley-Davidson Model WLDR

It's no secret that Harley-Davidson's reputation has been built primarily by the inimitable big V-twins (1000 cc and up) the company has produced for nearly a century. But a smaller powerplant—the 45-cubic-inch (750-cc)

side-valve V-twin—was the heart of Harley-Davidson's popular "Forty-Fives," launched in 1928 to answer Indian's Scout and Excelsior's Super-X. Harley's original total-loss-oiled Forty-Five evolved into the famous W series, whose various models remained in production until 1952.

Represented by this 1940 WLDR "race job," the rugged WL cruised comfortably at 60 mph. This bike was rebuilt in the 1980s and is currently raced by Michigan's Al Knapp, whose 50-year pro career began in 1947 with a crash that broke his arm and shoulder. In the game for over half a century, the septuagenarian Knapp is perhaps the most senior motorcycle racer in America, and he regularly competes aboard this 1940 specimen.

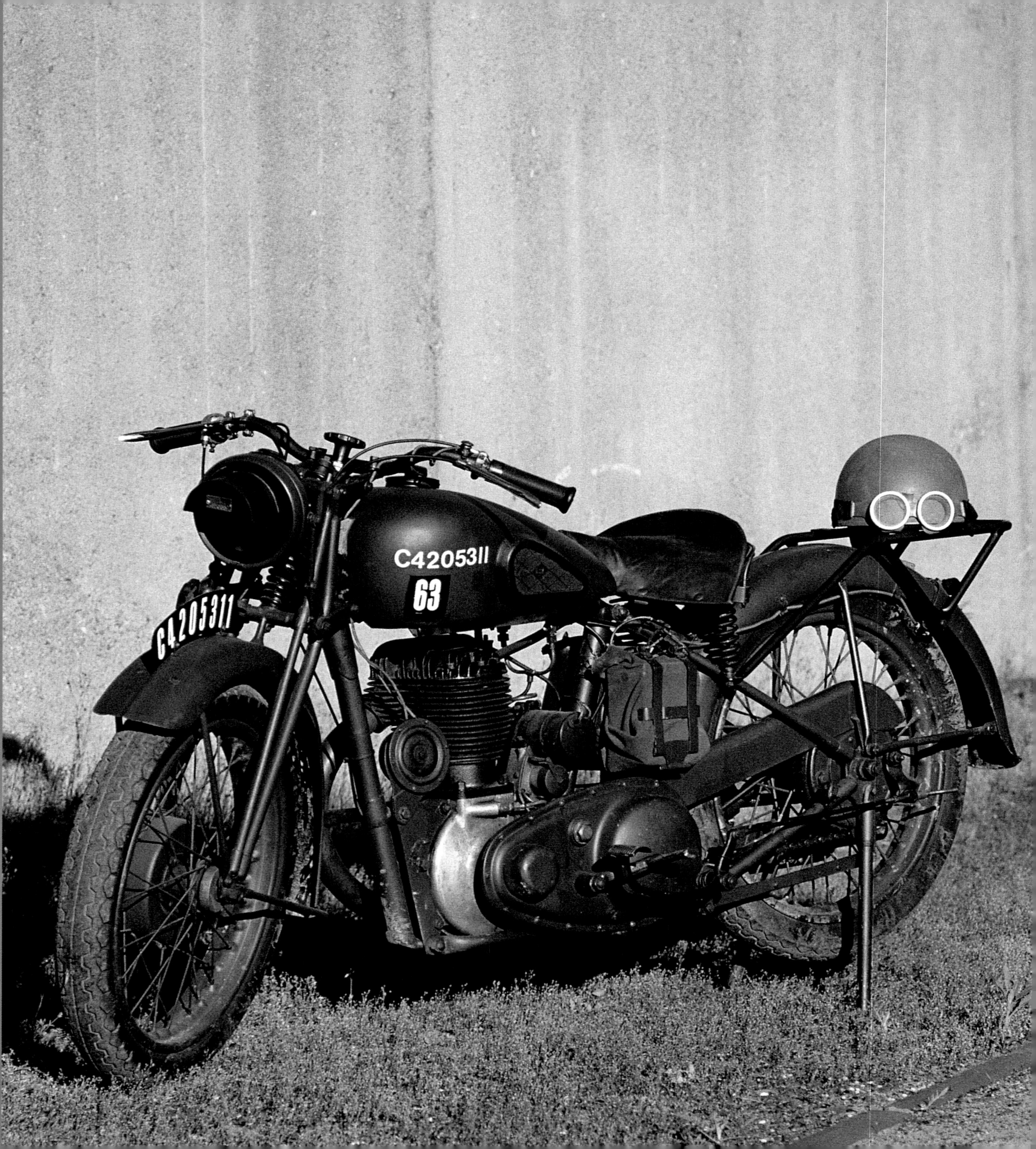
C4205311
63
C4205311

1941
BSA
WM20

Countless tons of bombs raining down on England during the Blitz of 1940 didn't deter British industry from supplying a large percentage of the motorcycles used by Allied troops during World War II. As one of Britain's largest producers of motorcycles and munitions, it fell to Birmingham Small Arms, along with competitors Norton, Matchless, and Triumph, to manufacture bikes for the war effort. Despite heavy bomb damage and loss of workers' lives, BSA came through with flying colors, turning out Britain's premiere wartime motorcycle, the M20.

Over 125,000 units of BSA's 500-cc single-cylinder M20 served with Allied forces around the globe. This original 1941 WM20, which performed dispatch duties and bears the markings of an armored unit of Welsh Guards, is shown with a blackout cover on its headlamp and a military rider's helmet on its cargo rack. A rugged workhorse, the M20 delivered yeoman's service, whether slogging through a muddy ford or whisking across parched desert sands.

1942
Harley-Davidson
Model WLA

As German mechanized forces rolled across Europe before America's entry into World War II, U.S. military planners began to recognize the need for a series of dependable vehicles to replace the horse in the modern cavalry. They requested designs for a 500-cc motorcycle from both Indian and Harley-Davidson. H-D's Arthur Davidson scoffed at the bike's small size, however, and instead developed a cheaper, hardier military version of the popular 45-cubic-inch (737-cc) V-twin WL. Designated the WLA, it became the best Allied motorcycle of World War II, with over 90,000 seeing action in every theater of the war.

A host of special modifications made the rugged, reliable WLA the ideal military motorcycle, as seen on this restored 1942 U.S. Army version: front and back blackout lights; extra-wide fenders; forward-mounted saddle; heavy-duty cargo carrier; extended bash plate; leg shield; olive-drab paint scheme; and, of course, a deadly Thompson 45-caliber submachine gun nestled in the fork-mounted scabbard!

1943-1944

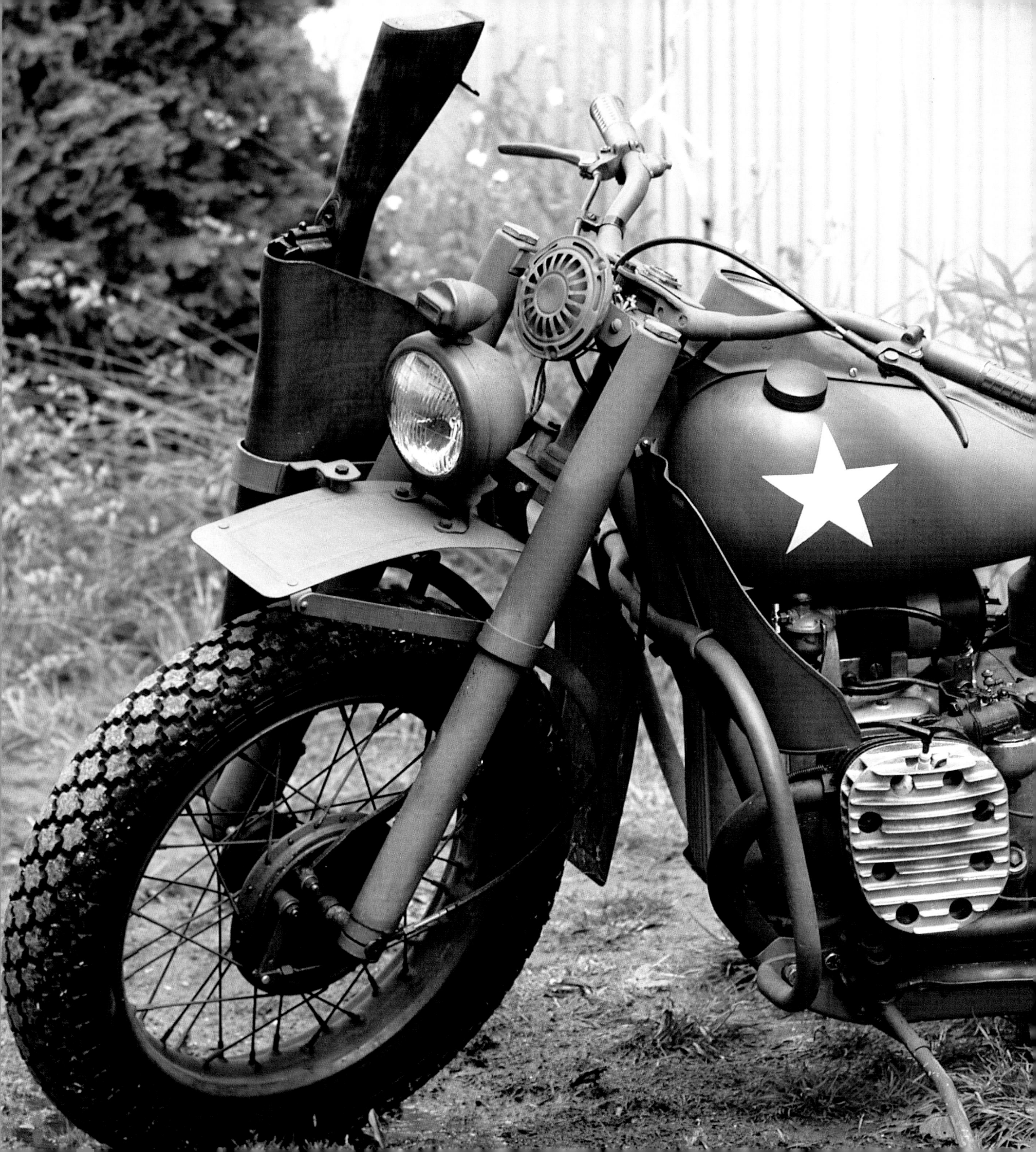

1943
Harley-Davidson
Model X2

While doing its bit to help the Allies win World War II, Harley-Davidson also helped itself—to a majority of the U.S. Army motorcycle contracts issued during the conflict. This, naturally, was welcome ammunition in Harley's own "war" with long-standing rival Indian, from which the Springfield company would never fully recover.

Along with its workhorse WLA model (see 1942), of which about 100,000 were built, the Milwaukee plant contributed a small number of other models to the fight. These included the Model U (see 1945), and the Model X2. Shown here in the U.S. Army configuration used between 1942 and 1945, the X2 was powered by a transverse-mounted, flat-twin side-valve engine, and driven by a shaft drive to the rear wheel. Like other wartime Harleys, the it served with distinction throughout the world.

1944
BMW R-71

Germany's Bayerische Motoren Werke—known internationally as BMW, and still among the most respected builders of cars and motorcycles in the world—unveiled its 500-cc R-32 flat-twin motorcycle in 1923, and it has only improved upon its masterful basic design ever since. During World War II, however, the company's Munich plant built bikes for the German war machine, including this military descendant of the R-32, the R-71, which was produced throughout the war.

The authentically restored 1938 BMW R-71 and sidecar featured here reportedly served with the Nazi SS in a POW camp in Poland from 1939 to 1945. Acquired by an American collector several years ago, the machine was rebuilt in Germany and cosmetically restored in the United States, and it carries recreated SS markings and original plates. It is maintained in running condition and still attains speeds of up to 60 mph. And the bike's converted MG-34 machine gun uses oxygen and propane to simulate the sound and flame originally produced by the weapon—resulting in a close call for the owner when a passerby thought the gun was shooting real ammunition!

1945
Harley-Davidson
Model U
(U.S. Navy)

Compared to the nearly 100,000 45-cubic-inch WLA motorcycles Harley-Davidson produced for United Nations forces in World War II, the production run of Harley's 74-cubic-inch Military Model U was relatively small. In fact, during 1944, when this particular bike was manufactured for the U.S. Navy, only 366 of these 74-cubic-inch V-twins were built.

Its low numbers, however, belie the value of this rugged military machine, which is based on the formidable side-valve 74-incher that Harley-Davidson began producing for the civilian market in 1930. As this expertly restored example attests, the Model U featured Harley's usual power and dependability, enhanced by a string of extras that made the bike unique not only from H-D's popular civilian models, but from its special police motorcycles as well. Painted in the Navy's usual flat, battleship-gray color scheme and originally assigned to shore-patrol duties, this historic bike sports blackout covers on both its fore and aft lights; a leather scabbard (holding a Thompson submachine gun) and dispatch pouches; heavy-duty carbs and filters; and authentic markings that indicate its service at a Naval Air Station.

1946
Harley-Davidson
Model WL

At the end of World War II, thousands of returning American G.I.'s exhibited a marked enthusiasm for motorcycling, often converting "retired" military WLA's for civilian use. Wishing to capitalize on this encouraging trend, Harley-Davidson decided to extend the series of 45-cubic-inch (750-cc) "W" machines when production of civilian motorcycles resumed after the war. Prominent among these was the Model WL, a sporty take on the basic W—with its air-cooled "knucklehead" V-twin engine—that made the most of a higher compression rate and the increased horsepower.

This detail is from a gleaming red restoration of a 1946 Harley-Davidson WL, "pieced together" by 50-year racing veteran Al Knapp. Rebuilding the bike from the bare frame up, Knapp re-bored the engine; added new pistons, valves, and valve guides; reworked the three-speed transmission; replaced the chains, battery, fenders, and tires; and re-chromed the plated parts. The result is a marvelous example of a postwar Harley—pleasing to the eye and a joy to ride.

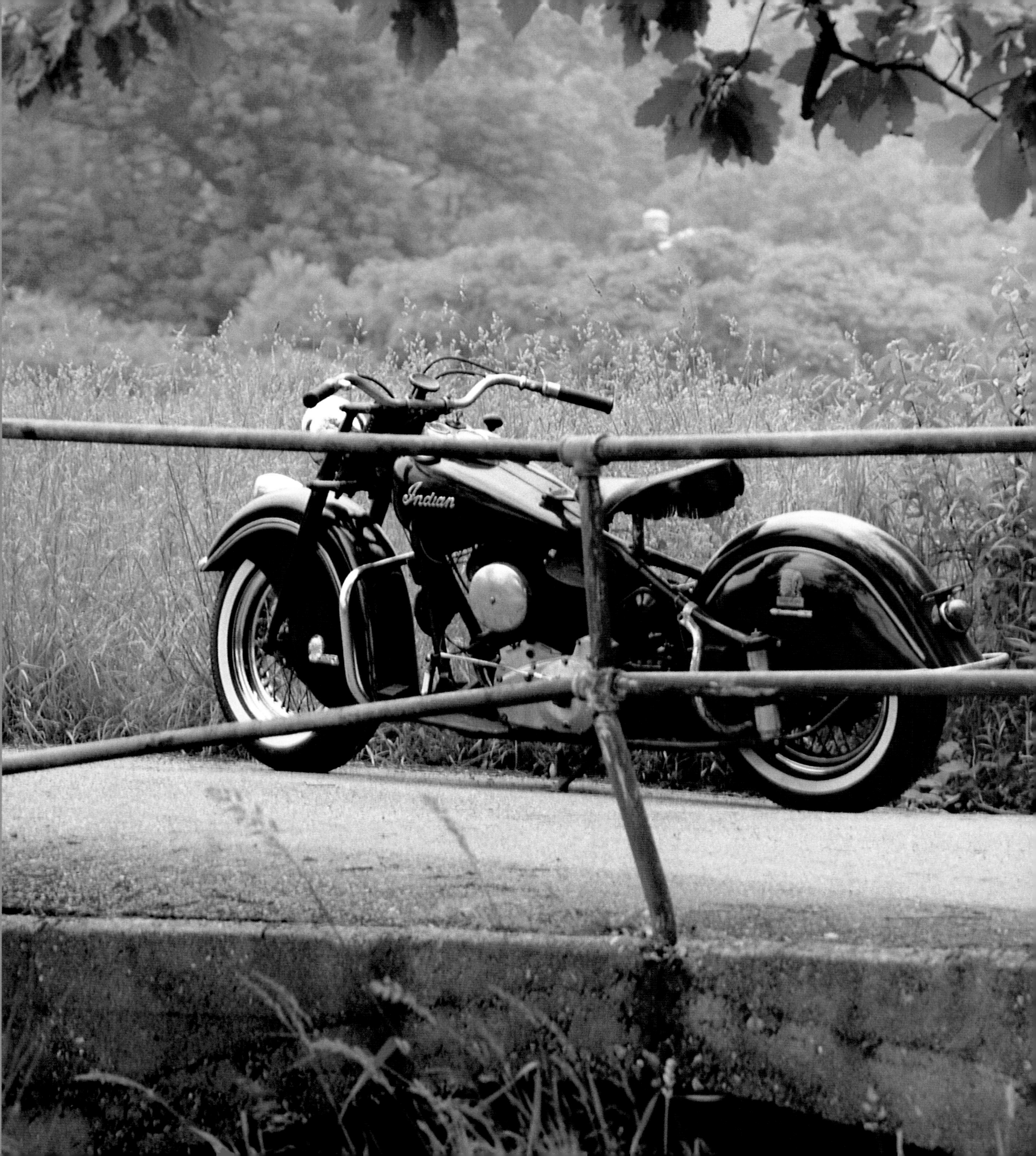
Indian

1947
Indian Chief

The year 1947 was a good one for the Indian Chief—as least as far as styling goes. Sure, the 1947 Chief's big 74-cubic-inch (1213-cc) V-twin ran reliably enough, as most Indian engines did. The bike's considerable heft, however—about 550 pounds—rendered its speed and acceleration inferior to that of comparable Harley-Davidsons, the only American competition. And its original small drum-brake was barely enough to stop a machine of its bulk.

But the 1947 Chief was certainly a looker, as this unrestored black beauty illustrates. The generous skirted fenders (introduced in 1940), attractive instrumentation, sleek tank design, girder forks, and illuminated Indian mascot all contributed to the motorcycle's image of streamlined luxury.

1948
Vincent/HRD
Black Lightning
"Bathing Suit Bike"

This Vincent/HRD has a secure place in motorcycling history. At a dinner meeting in May of 1948, a Los Angeles Vincent dealer named B.L. Martin approached Vincent/HRD chief Philip Vincent with a proposal: Martin wanted a Vincent/HRD motorcycle to beat the standing ocean-level land-speed record of 137 mph, set by Joe Petrali on a tuned Harley-Davidson 61 in 1937. Vincent agreed to supply the bike.

The machine—an alcohol-fueled, tuned 1948 Black Lightning V-twin that had tested at 143 mph—was delivered on August 27 to 48-year-old Rollie Free, the Indy-500 race driver who would make the attempt. Two weeks later, on September 13, at the Bonneville Salt Flats, Free made a run of 148 mph. Anxious to top 150, Rollie stripped down to swim trunks and assumed a prone position that enabled him to set a world record at 150.313 mph. The photo of Rollie's feat gained worldwide fame—as did the "bathing suit bike" itself, seen here restored and exhibited by the Vincent Owners Club.

1949

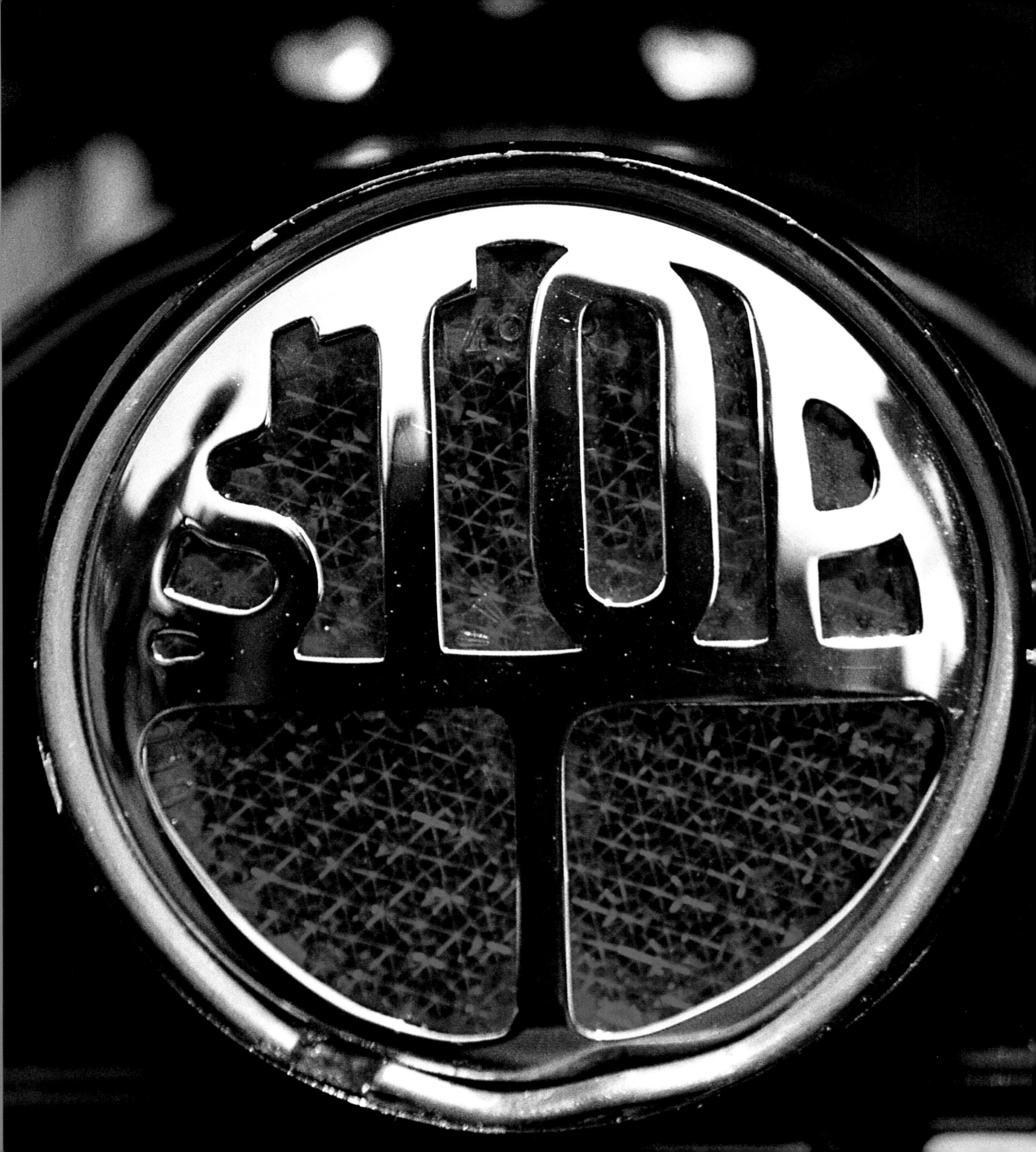

1949
Vincent/HRD
Series B

The genesis of the legendary
Vincent/HRD marque is a fascinating
one. In 1928, young engineer and
Cambridge student Philip Vincent
bought the bankrupt cycle company
founded four years earlier by TT
racer Howard R. Davies. Over the
next 20 years, Vincent developed a
series of progressively improved high-
performance motorcycles under the
"Vincent/HRD" banner, initially
using JAP engines. The first Vincent
engine appeared in the mid-thirties, a

500-cc single that was later "doubled
up" into the marque's renowned
1000-cc V-twins.

All of Vincent's machines employed
the cantilever rear suspension system
he had designed at school, and most
were among the fastest and safest
motorcycles of their time. This

restored Series B, featuring the V-
twin as part of the chassis, is from the
"transition year" 1949, after which the
"HRD" was finally dropped to avoid
confusion with "H-D" (Harley-
Davidson). In the early fifties, this
very bike regularly took on Indians
and Harleys in illegal midnight races
on Brooklyn's Belt Parkway.

1950-1959

Big, brash, and rebellious—
the motorcycle takes on a whole
new image in the postwar world.
For some, two-wheeled transport
is a daily necessity; for others, it's
simply a lark. But the market is
changing. Suddenly, the once-
mighty Indian is no more, and
great British machines cruise
merrily along, while Japanese
bikes move up from behind.

1950
Indian Chief Custom

The "Fabulous Fifties" was a golden age of elaborate styling and personal expression on the American road, producing the "hot rod," the customizing craze, and some of the biggest, brashest cars and motorcycles ever built. So it's fitting that "Wild Bill" Eggers' remarkable personalization of a 1950 Indian Chief represents the first year of that incredible decade.

As he did with his 1930 Indian Four seen elsewhere in this book, Eggers abandoned his usual penchant for authenticity and let his imagination—and a passion for Native American imagery—run wild throughout this 1950 Chief. Wild Bill's personal mark permeates this bike, from the

intricately tooled and beaded leatherwork to the southwestern graphics he spent months designing himself. Chrome gleams throughout the Chief's massive 80-cubic-inch engine, and stretches from the fender trim to the ball-topped fishtail exhausts.

This machine won Eggers a "Best Custom" award at Daytona, and ranks among the finest custom bikes in the world. Valued in the six figures, it demonstrates that a great motorcycle truly is a work of art.

1951

1951
Indian Chief
Roadmaster

The thirty-year history of the mighty Indian Chief reached its pinnacle—just a few short years before its untimely end in 1953— with the majestic 1951 Roadmaster. In three decades the Chief had grown considerably from the debut 1000-cc model of 1922, created by Scout designer C.B. Franklin. Even when compared to the first 1200-cc "Big Chief," introduced in 1923, the 1951 Roadmaster seems massive—and it is. Powered by an 80-cubic-inch (1320-cc) V-twin, it weighs in at over 600 pounds, making it the heaviest Indian in history. And all that bulk, along with superior engineering, made for a very smooth ride.

The beautifully restored 1952 Chief shown here sports a long bench seat and a fishtail exhaust in addition to the features that made the 1951 Chief a legend: the lighted Indian head on the front fender; telescoping front forks; the huge V-twin engine; the big skirted fenders; the proud script tank badge. It's all there, and all Indian Chief.

1952
Vincent Rapide
Series C

One may use "remarkable," "exceptional," or some similar adjective to describe the Vincent Rapide Series C, and never be far from the truth. Produced from 1949 to 1954, the Series C Rapide improved upon the innovations of the earlier Series B. Its air-cooled 1000-cc, 50-degree V-twin powerplant enabled it to reach 100 mph in a heartbeat. Combining tremendous performance with superb handling and braking, this stunning machine epitomized Vincent's quest to produce the world's finest motorbike. In fact, the Black Shadow—a tuned version of the Rapide with improved cosmetics, engine detailing, and instrumentation—claimed the title of "the world's fastest and safest standard motorcycle."

With 20,000 miles on it, this award-winning restoration of a 1952 Rapide Series C is only slightly less resplendent than when first rebuilt. It's regularly ridden long-distance by its owner and can comfortably cruise today's highways at 80 mph—one of the few vintage bikes capable of such a feat.

1953
Zundapp KS 601

Originally founded to manufacture artillery fuses during World War I, the Zundapp factory in Nuremberg, Germany, began six decades of motorcycle production in the 1920s. The firm's first machines were two-stroke singles known for their reliability. In the 1930s Zundapp added flat-twins and flat-fours to its repertoire, and by mid-decade had produced its 100,000th motorcycle. Like BMW and other German cycle makers, the factory turned out such wartime military machines as the KS 600 and KS 750, and then produced sporting flat-twins and two-strokes after the war.

Typical of Zundapp's postwar output is the KS 601, introduced in 1951 and dubbed the "Green Elephant." Propelled by a 598-cc, horizontally opposed, overhead-valve twin engine, this sporty bike featured a chain-drive transmission. This remarkably well-preserved, unrestored KS 601 was purchased from its German owner, who covered it in grease and stored it for a quarter-century. The current American owner cleaned it up, and —voila!—an instant German classic.

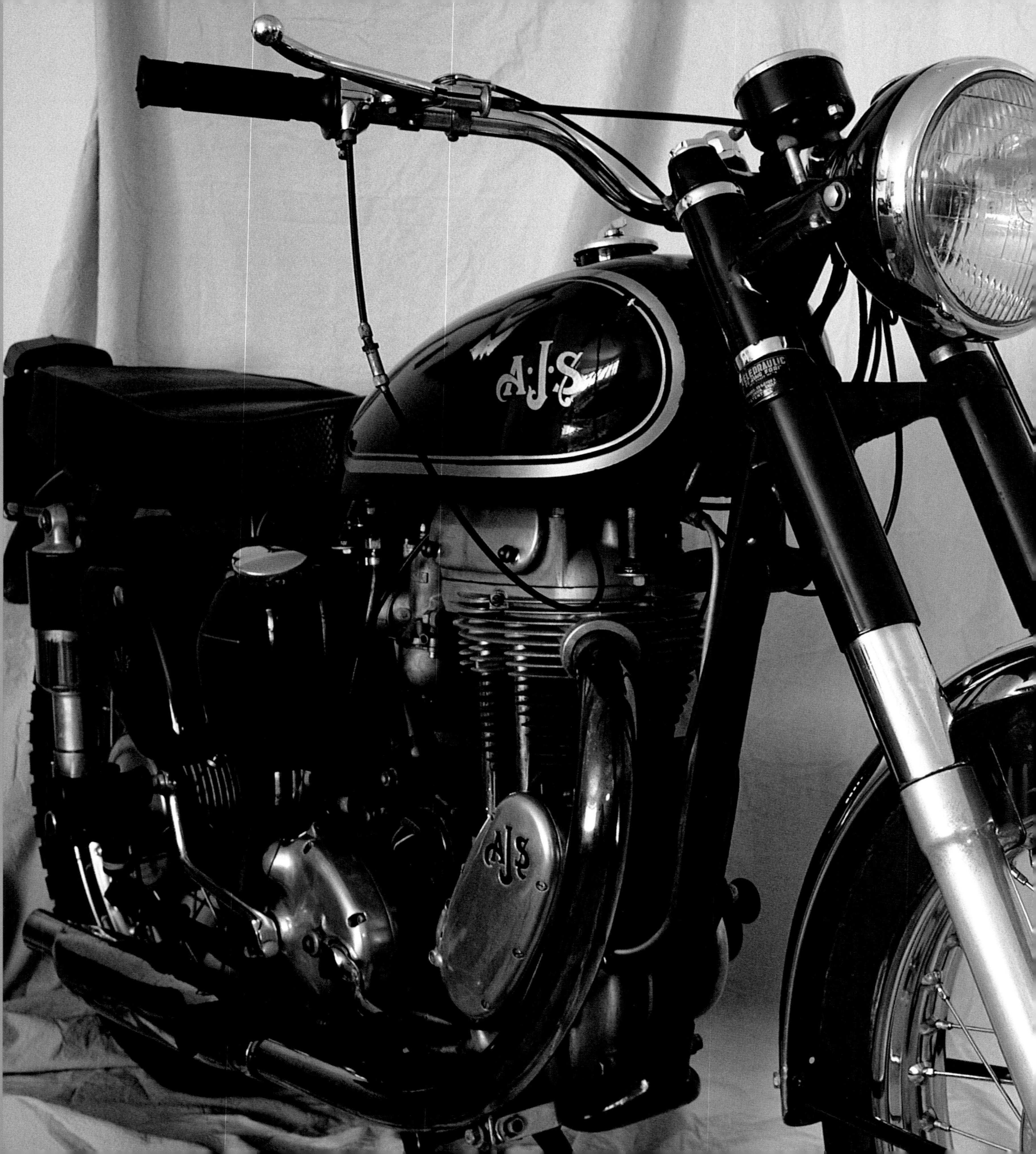
A·J·S
AJS

1954
AJS 18 CS

Launched with a 298-cc side-valve single designed and built by brothers George, Harry, Jack, and Joe Stevens in 1909, the British AJS marque survived for nearly six decades, despite a string of ownership changes through the years. By the mid-1950s, AJS had joined Matchless and Norton as part of Associated Motor Cycles, Ltd.—at that time, the largest cycle maker in the world.

Sporting squat rear shock absorbers that gave rise to its nickname, "jampot," the restored 1954 18 CS seen here is a road version of the AJS dirt scrambler popular with adventurous riders in both the U.K. and the U.S. in the fifties and sixties. When fitted with the proper tires and equipment, this sturdy 500-cc single was a go-anywhere, do-anything kind of bike. The speedy, maneuverable 18 CS was a common sight wherever dirt-bike enthusiasts would gather to do their stuff—from the California desert to the English hills.

1955
Triumph Tiger 110

Following in the tracks of designer Edward Turner's legendary 1937 Speed Twin, Triumph unleashed a year later the Tiger 100—a sporty mount that, with a bit of luck, really could hit the 100-mph mark. Enjoying brisk sales right through to the 1950s, the Tiger, which had by mid-decade become the 110, possessed both the looks and the performance to epitomize the fast, frenzied popular culture of the "Fabulous Fifties."

The sleek lines of this gleaming black-framed and seashell-blue 1955 Tiger speak volumes about the importance of styling to the burgeoning postwar motorcycle market. Speed, of course, was also a long-standing Tiger tradition. This Tiger sports a powerful 650-cc engine of the type that Johnny Allen modified to set a new unofficial motorcycle speed record of 214.4 mph in 1956. In fact, not only did the gorgeous Tiger 110 hold its own against competition from all comers, it also spawned the most famous Triumph of all—the Bonneville 120—which took its name from the famous Utah salt flats where Allen made his record run.

1956
Ariel Square Four

In 1930, Britain's Ariel introduced a new model that represented a radical departure from the well-made but rather conventional singles the company had specialized in since the turn of the century. It was the extraordinary Square Four: a four-cylinder 500-cc machine utilizing a sophisticated "square"-cylinder configuration and a single overhead camshaft. Incorporating two crankshafts with two twin cylinders in a square formation, designer Edward Turner created a powerful four that was light enough to fit into a single's frame. Affectionately known as the "Squariel," various versions of it would sell successfully for nearly 30 years.

Here is an all-original 1000-cc 1956 Square Four, featuring an all-aluminum engine, four individual exhaust pipes, and a top-yoke-mounted speedometer. The owner of this remarkable bike originally purchased it in 1963, sold it in 1978, regretted it—and bought it back 18 years later, after his son discovered the very same bike languishing in a shop!

1957
Simplex Automatic

Throughout motorcycle history, several distinctly different makes have carried the same name. Excelsior was such a case; so was Simplex. There were at least four distinctive Simplex marques: a leading Dutch make produced between 1902 and 1968; a 1920s British manufacturer of two-stroke bicycle attachment engines; a handsome compact cycle designed and built in Italy from 1921 to 1950; and the American Simplex represented here, manufactured in New Orleans from the late thirties to the late sixties.

A lightweight machine intended for short distances, the Simplex had a crankshaft supported by only one main bearing, and a rather weak 125-cc engine. The owner of this 1956 Automatic restored it from a "basket case," adding a 150-cc powerplant and such original "extras" as speedometer, front brake, and horn. He describes the Simplex as a bike that will "run well if you run it right," calling it "one of the flavors everybody else doesn't have."

1958
Moto Guzzi
SuperAlce

The name Moto Guzzi evokes a long tradition of excellence in motorcycle design, dating from the company's World War I origins. Two Italian Air Corps pilots, Giorgio Parodi and Giovanni Ravelli, planned to found a motorcycle company with their mechanic, Carlo Guzzi. While Ravelli was killed in action, Parodi and Guzzi survived to establish their firm, and they chose the air corps' eagle logo to honor their fallen friend. Over the next four decades, Moto Guzzi became Italy's largest cycle maker, enjoying great success with its excellent 500-cc flat singles.

In 1947 the company introduced the SuperAlce, the last of the open-valve Guzzis. A four-speed, 500-cc horizontal single with a top speed of 70 mph, it remained in production until 1958, and is represented here by an unrestored 1950 two-seater used by a Milan fire department as a scout/escort vehicle until 1997. When its current American owner removed it from its crate, the 48-year-old machine started on the second kick!

1959
BMW Single

Manufacturing only aircraft engines until after World War I, German giant BMW produced its first complete motorcycle in 1923—a 500-cc machine designed by Max Friz, with a crankshaft running the length of the bike, and the cylinders protruding to the

side. This flat-twin configuration has been the mainstay of BMW ever since, and the company has built a 75-year business on the strength of its success.

But BMW has also created well-regarded motorcycles that don't rely on the firm's classic flat-twin design—at least not entirely. The BMW Single, produced until 1967, actually "borrows" from the popular flat-twin engine by employing one cylinder from the twin and mounting it vertically into the frame. A smaller bike than the famous twin, the Single uses the same crankshaft configuration. The gleaming white BMW Single shown here is a 1959 version, and it is often used with a sidecar.

1960
Triton

It's rather difficult to follow the permutations of the United Kingdom's postwar motorcycle industry—and the "cannibalization" of famous British marques—without a program. In the 1940s, Ariel became part of BSA, and in the 1950s, BSA bought Triumph, and Norton joined AJS and Matchless in AMC. Then, in the 1960s, BSA/Triumph combined with Norton to form the Norton-Villiers-Triumph Group, which by the 1970s controlled all British motorcycle production.

Amidst all this shuffling emerged a motorcycle with a short but curious history. Represented by this rebuilt 1960 machine, Triton was not a marque in itself, but a unique "special"

created by combining Norton's slimline "featherbed" frame with the Triumph Bonneville's classic 649-cc parallel-twin engine. The result, one of the best-known café racers of the 1960s, was the Triton—part Triumph, part Norton.

With his London-based Dresda Engineering, British engineer and one-time racer Dave Degens was a major advocate of the Triton in the 1960s, and he has been building and racing similar machines ever since.

1960-1969

In America, Harley-Davidson stands alone as the decade begins. Stiff competition comes from the British, who dominate the world market, and the Japanese, who want to. Honda's little Super Cub becomes the best-selling bike in history, Harley "choppers" take styling to the extreme, and Britain's cycle makers play musical chairs.

1961
Harley-Davidson
KR750 Racer

After a half-century of developing and racing competition motorcycles, Harley-Davidson had come a long way from that first Harley "racer" ridden by Walter Davidson in 1909. By the dawn of the 1960s, with its chief American rival, Indian, now just a memory, the Motor Company's racing program was kept busy meeting the challenges presented by a slew of new competitors from Japan and Europe. And the bike that carried the Harley banner for much of that time was the KR750 and its dirt-track version, the KRTT.

The quintessential Harley road-racing machine, from its debut in 1952 to its "retirement" in the late 1960s, the KR750 initially drew its speed from a side-valve 45-degree V-twin displacing 750 cc (45 cubic inches), generating about 50 bhp. Overhead-valve engines replaced side-valves in road bikes after 1955, but Harley stuck with the KR750's design until unveiling its overhead-valve successor, the XR750, in 1968.

This beautiful blue KR750, restored to a 1960 road-racing configuration, is similar to the bike that Roger Reiman rode to victory in the 1961 Daytona 200-mile race.

1962
Panther Stroud

The Panther marque was originally called P & M and marketed as "The Perfected Motorcycle"—although the letters actually stood for Jonah Phelon and Richard Moore, who founded the company in 1900. Like a number of other venerable British cycle makers, Panther developed some V-twin machines. But the marque made its name with well-made singles, surviving into the mid-1960s with a series of bikes that, while not particularly fast, were especially good at pulling a sidecar.

Pioneering a sloping, forward-leaning engine configuration in some of their earliest motorcycles, P & M/Panther made gradual improvements to their basic design over the years. But much like Germany's BMW, Panther found something that worked and stuck with it. The 100S, Panther's popular 598-cc workhorse, changed comparatively little from its introduction in 1928 to its last version in the 1960s. And later models on the road in 1962, like this 1950 Panther Stroud, also display roots that go all the way back to the turn-of-the-century P & M "slopers."

1963
BSA
B44 VE

In the shadow of the threat posed to the British marques by competitive Japanese bikes, the Birmingham Small Arms Company celebrated its centennial in 1963. BSA had been in the motorcycle business for more than half its 100 years, and for a time in the fifties was the largest cycle maker in the world. But as the sixties rolled on, things were changing quickly.

Like other British companies, BSA had always counted on its pedigree and its superior single and twin machines—such as this beautiful 1964 BSA B44 VE—to beat back foreign competition. But when that strategy failed and the Japanese grabbed the small-bike market, British makers felt their vaunted "big machines" would win the day. Again, they were wrong —and although BSA and its allied marques would survive the sixties, the end was in sight.

1964
Harley-Davidson
Electra-Glide

Time rolls on... and so do Harley-Davidson's inimitable FL 1200-cc (74-cubic-inch) V-twins, still "gliding" after five decades of development. The legendary Milwaukee factory continually improved the initial "Panhead" powerplant after its post-war debut, introducing a string of famous models that each put a new twist on the popular machine.

It began in 1949 with the Hydra-Glide, named for its new hydraulic front suspension, and continued with 1958's Duo-Glide, whose considerable power was complemented by the addition of rear shocks. Then, in 1964, the Motor Company unveiled what many still consider the classic American touring bike, whose name refers to the first electric starter in Harley-Davidson's history—the Electra-Glide.

As this 1965 original shows, the first Electra-Glide was as beautiful as it was beefy, featuring the last Panhead engine and employing an eight-speed transmission. Among the greatest of the firm's postwar bikes, it has earned a special place in Harley history.

1965

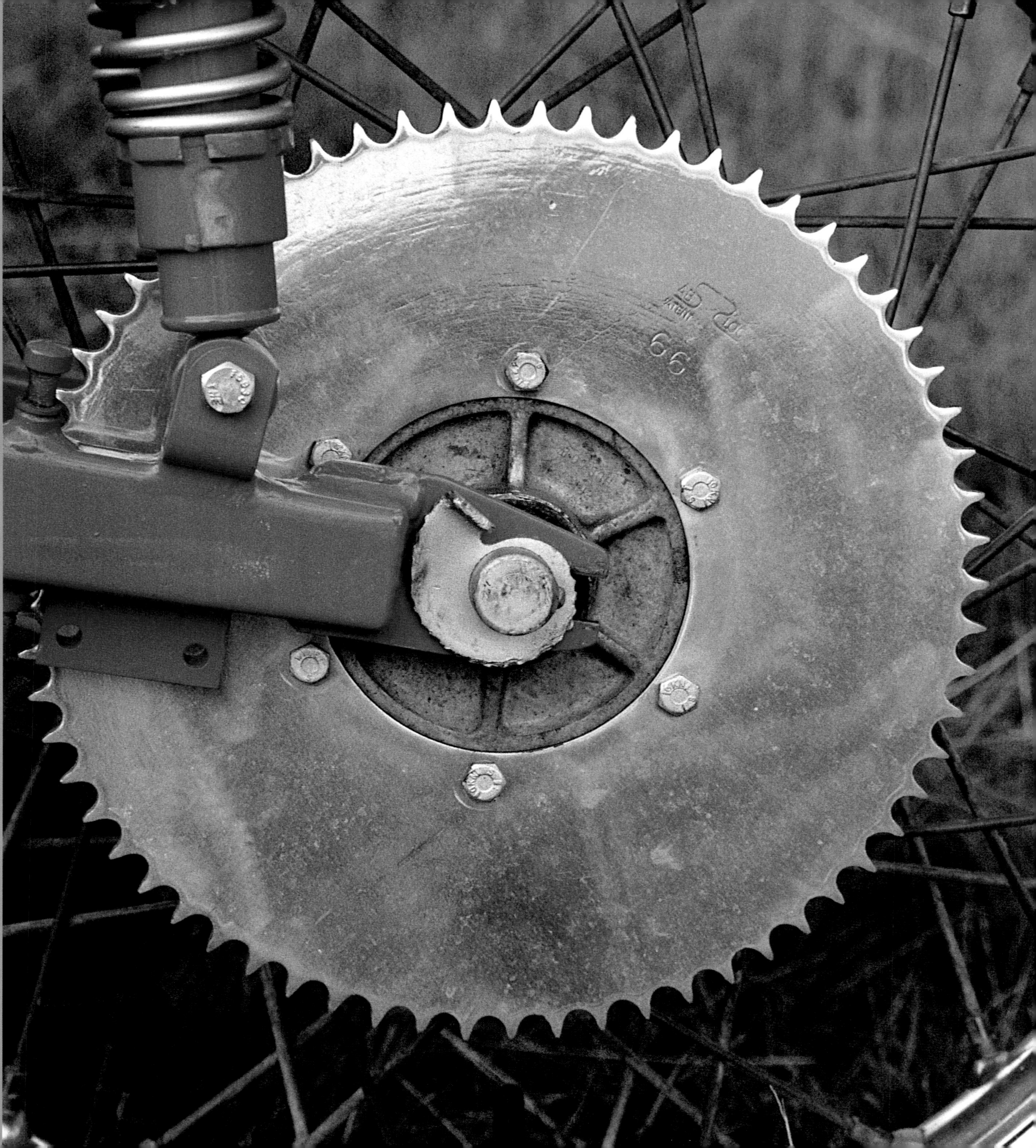

1965
Greeves Algean

The British firm founded by former invalid-carriage manufacturing executive O.B. (Bert) Greeves in 1952 immediately gained a reputation for producing light roadsters of superior quality. Greeves' unorthodox ideas about suspension and frame design—often incorporating a combined steering head and front downmember of cast alloy, with leading-link forks and rubber suspension—are especially evident in his unique trials bikes, which compiled an impressive record in competition in the fifties and sixties. The company's later output concentrated on machines designed primarily for trials and cross-country racing.

Described as irresistibly "cute" by its owner—who obtained it in a trade and decided to keep it—the 1965 Greeves Algean (named for a trials competition) seen here was rebuilt from original parts. Powered by a 250-cc Villiers two-stroke engine incorporating a Greeves-designed top-end, this unusual bike is a fine example of the well-engineered, painstakingly finished machines for which Greeves became famous.

1966
Norton Atlas 750

Proud and unvarying, the Norton logo adorned the traditional silver tanks of many excellent overhead-cam singles from the late 1920s to the early 1960s. The first of these appeared in 1927—the 25th anniversary of British engineer James Landsdowne Norton's first motorcycle in 1902. The slogan "the Unapproachable Norton" echoed the high performance of the marques' singles and parallel-twins. Even the names exuded confidence: Dominator, Atlas, Commando, and Manx.

In 1950, Norton engineers designed a double-loop tubular steel frame that greatly improved handling. A test rider remarked that it felt like "riding a featherbed." The name stuck, and the Featherbed frame played a major role in Norton's success.

Norton's Atlas 750, a 745-cc parallel twin, first appeared in 1964. Represented here by a pristine 1966 example, this formidable bike suffered from its big twin's excessive vibration. Norton's design team responded with the Isolastic rubber engine-mount system, and introduced it in the Commando, which replaced the Atlas.

1967
Honda Twin

The industrial giant Honda began, humbly enough, in a small wooden shed in Hamamatsu, Japan. In 1946, a blacksmith's son, Soichiro Honda, began supplying his war-shattered country with cheap daily transportation by fitting bicycles with Army-surplus engines. By 1949 he had built his first complete motorcycle, the two-stroke 98-cc Model D "Dream."

Within 10 years, Honda had not only become Japan's leading motorcycle producer, but had also begun exporting its bikes, like 1958's reliable little C100 Super Cub, to the U.S. and elsewhere. Capitalizing on its wholesome image—"You meet the nicest people on a Honda," the ads went—the Super Cub eventually became the best-selling motorcycle of all time.

Early Hondas, including the first parallel-twins, employed pressed-steel frames and leading-link front forks. But as the marque moved into the 1960s, bigger machines, like the 305-cc CB77 and 1965's CB450, had begun featuring tubular frames and telescopic forks, as is illustrated by the restored 1967 Honda twin model shown here.

1968
BMW R69/2

Clean, functional styling... impeccable craftsmanship... gradual improvements made to an already sound basic design. Anyone familiar with BMW motorcycles would easily recognize those hallmarks of the Bayerische Motoren Werke's output throughout its long history. Every "Beemer" bike introduced since the company began has strong ties to that very first flat-twin of 1928. The R69, seen here in its 1968 edition (although with a 1975 engine) and accompanied by a Ural sidecar, was no exception.

A comparison between the earliest BMW twin and this machine, created 40 years later, will naturally yield numerous differences due to improved technologies over the decades. But it is the similarities that are so striking: the same basic engine design and its protruding heads; the same black paint scheme; the same logo and striping on the fuel tank; the same attention to detail throughout. It's almost as if the BMW motto was "if it's not broken, don't fix it." And since the R69/2 and its forerunners seem to go on forever with only slight modifications, the philosophy appears to be working.

1969 Honda Composite Racer

One veteran motorcycle racer has remarked: "The really true 'race jobs' are built in the basement; after we'd get 'em, we'd take 'em down and go to work on 'em... then they went fast." In the case of this Honda composite racer, however, Californian Brent Hensley really started from scratch— with "a $100 junk bike; the only thing stock on it is the crankshaft."

Customizing this "race job" from that crankshaft up, Hensley used a late-sixties Honda 450-cc engine punched out to 518 cc, with a cylinder head from the bike that won the 1994 Daytona. He added titanium axles and fasteners, homemade brackets, a 400-F tank, a BSA fender, a Suzuki front-end, and fairings from Northern Ireland. Then he painted the motorcycle himself, inspired by a model of a CR-1000 French Endurance Team bike. Finally, 18 months after he'd begun, Hensley finished off his "race job" with various decals and stickers (helped by his young daughter), and raced it at the Mid-Ohio course the day after these photos were taken.

OVERLEAF

From road-racing events and natural-terrain motocross to trials, TT, dirt-track, hill-climbing, drag-race, speedway, and even ice-racing competition, motorcycle sport has thrived since the very beginning of the century.

1970
Triumph T120
Custom

A motorcycle's heart is its engine—the mass of moving metal parts that not only propels the machine, but defines it as well. Motorcycle design is usually expressed in terms of engine design; bikes are referred to as "singles," "V-twins," "Fours," etc. And when it comes to custom motorcycles, the engine is often the only means of identifying what a particular machine is—or what it once was.

Take this radical custom "chopper." Its 649-cc parallel-twin heart was "donated" by a 1970 Triumph T120 Bonneville—an enhanced version of the T110 (see 1955), which descended from the 498-cc Speed Twin of 1937.

"Radical" may not adequately describe how this motorcycle has been transformed into a one-of-a-kind dream machine. The frame is shortened and angled, and the seat is mounted onto the fender above the small rear tire. An outrageously long "corkscrew" front fork is raked back in a classic sixties chopper configuration, and it is fitted with an oversize front tire. A closer look will reveal the many unique features of this splendid custom restoration.

1970

1970-1979

The "superbike" comes into its own, with Japan taking the lead from Britain, and the rest of Europe joining in. While Honda redefines touring with the Gold Wing, the British industry self-destructs; even Harley-Davidson finds itself struggling. And a bullet-shaped Kawasaki streaks across Bonneville at 318 mph, setting a new land-speed record.

1971 Harley-Davidson XLH Sportster

Through its nearly forty-year existence, the look of Harley-Davidson's Sportster has changed comparatively little, while performance is another story. Launched in 1957, the loud and powerful 883-cc XLCH Sportster quickly gained a reputation for living up to its name. By the early 1960s it ranked as one of the fastest bikes on the road, and had no problem topping 100 mph. Over the years, however, Harley increased the capacity from 883 cc to 1000 cc to 1200 cc, but the changes yielded little in the way of improved performance.

In 1986, Harley-Davidson introduced yet another Sportster with an 883-cc Evolution engine and continued producing the model into the 1990s. The machine seen here, however, began life in 1971 as a 1972 XLH Sportster. It was later customized with its 900-cc stock engine bored out to 1000 cc. Rebuilt over a six-month period, it's a prime example of how a lot of elbow grease can take a bike as far as an imagination will allow.

1972
Triumph Custom Hybrid

Carrying on the long-standing tradition begun in 1937 with the legendary Speed Twin, Triumph continued to produce updated versions of its classic vertical overhead-valve machines right up to the 1980s. This one-of-a-kind bike pays tribute to that tradition, like a jazz version of a standard tune that honors the original but stands as a unique work in its own right.

Pieced together by Ohio restorer Bob Ward, this "mostly Triumph" custom hybrid features parts from various years and models. At its heart is a 1972 Triumph 650-cc vertical overhead-valve twin with electronic ignition and five-speed transmission, married to a 1970 front frame section and a 1974 disc-brake front-end. It features a 1964 gas tank, a T-150 fork top, and a T-160 fork tree. There are also Harley parts sprinkled throughout, and parts from numerous other manufacturers—including the forward controls, linkage, tailpipes, and engine plates.

1973
Honda Trail 90

The largest of Japan's "Big Four" motorcycle manufacturers, Honda had risen to a dominant position in the world market by the mid-1960s by building safe, economical, and fun-to-ride bikes with a wholesome image. As the company approached its 25th anniversary in 1973, it was already producing big machines like the four-cylinder CB750, introduced in 1968. But Honda never neglected the small-bike market that had fostered its early success, and it continued to build such little machines as the Trail 90, one of the first dual-purpose motorcycles.

Hailing from Honda's silver anniversary year, this original 1973 Trail 90 was the perfect choice for sportsmen seeking a small, well-handling machine for on- or off-road use.

The trail bike's clutchless, dual-range transmission is favored by hunters for its ability to easily climb hills and scurry through woods. Although employed more often in an off-road capacity, this neat little 90-cc motorcycle is also suitable for the road, and capable of a top speed of around 45 mph.

水午

1974
Suzuki GT750

From an unlikely start as a maker of weaving equipment, the Japanese firm founded by Michio Suzuki in 1909 ventured into the motorbike business in 1952 with a 36-cc clip-on bicycle engine, and produced its first real motorcycle, a 125-cc two-stroke, three years later. Development of small two-strokes continued into the mid-sixties, when the company branched out into larger machines with the 500-cc parallel-twin T-500 in 1967.

Although it would switch to four-strokes later in the 1970s due to stringent emission-control regulations, Suzuki roared into the "superbike" market with its unconventional three-

cylinder, two-stroke GT750 in 1971. This rather bulky, water-cooled 738-cc machine earned the nickname "Kettle" in the U.K., and "Water Buffalo" in the States. Heavy and somewhat hard to handle, the GT750 nonetheless provided a smooth, quiet, comfortable ride—and its top speed of 115 mph was not too shabby. Represented here by a handsome, windshield-equipped 1974 model, the

"Water Buffalo" remained a popular sports-tourer throughout the decade, and paved the way for even more muscular Suzukis to come.

1975
Ural Sportsman 650

Motorcycling's history is full of fascinating little stories about these two-wheeled machines. The origin of the Ural sidecar motorcycle is just such a tale.

In the early days of World War II, a team of Red Army engineers disassembled five BMW motorcycles, copying their parts for duplication. They came up with the Ural, a simple "war bike" capable of negotiating rough terrain under battle conditions.

That was in 1939... and the Ural has remained in production ever since. All the Urals built over the past six decades are essentially the same bikes, assembled in the same town of Irbit, as were those first BMW "clones."

In 1975, thirty years after the end of the war, Urals were still rolling out of the factory for distribution primarily in the U.S.S.R. Since the Soviet Union's collapse in 1990, however, the marque has been exported to countries abroad, including the United States.

Powered by a 649-cc opposed-twin, four Ural models—including the 1995 Sportsman seen here—are equipped with sidecars; only the Solo, based on the 1950 BMW R60, is not.

1976

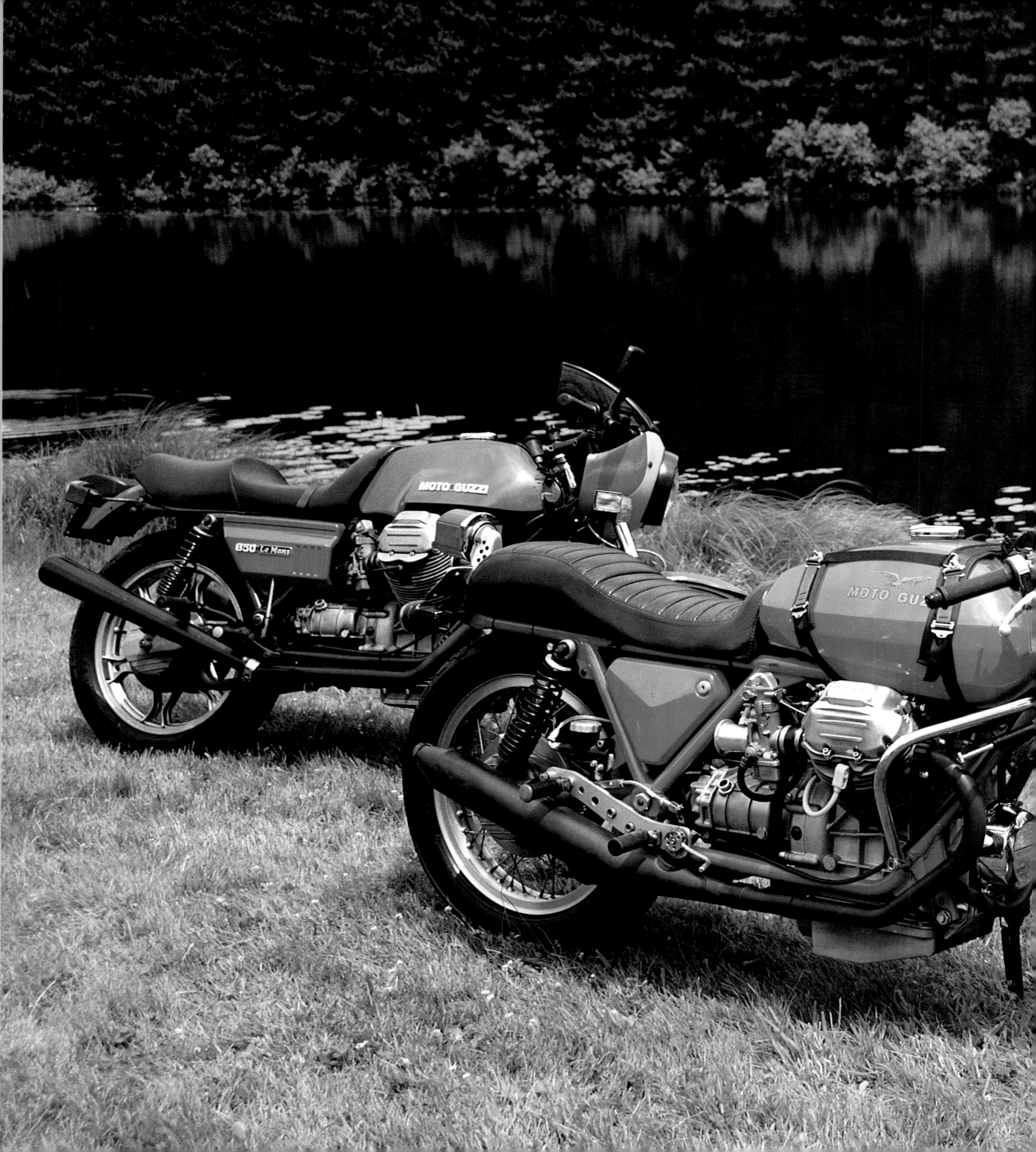

1976
Moto Guzzi LeMans
850 Custom

Unholy speed and elegant styling characterized the Moto Guzzi marque from its inception in the 1920s. A half-century later, a new Guzzi was still expected to be fast and sleek, even after the Italian company experienced difficulties in the early seventies.

In 1976, however, Moto Guzzi introduced a new model destined to become the firm's most beloved bike ever: the LeMans 850, two versions of which are featured here.

With a tuned, 844-cc 90-degree transverse twin boosted by high-compression pistons at its heart, the LeMans 850 was a lean, mean, but very clean machine with a 130-mph top end. The motorcycle's efficient shaft drive,

excellent handling, and effective braking combined with its power and café-racer styling to rank it among the finest superbikes of its day.

Both bikes shown originated in 1976, the LeMans' inaugural year. In the background is a pure MK I, while the machine in the foreground is actually a composite of the LeMans MK I, the V7 (launched in 1967), and the T3.

1977 Rickmann/ Triumph Custom Racer

Since the late 1950s, the company headed by the Rickmann brothers—at one time among Britain's leading motocross riders—has supplied excellent frames for customized motorcycles featuring such engines as Honda and Kawasaki fours, Nortons, and Triumph twins like the one showcased here. Starting with a 1967 Rickmann "Roadrace Metisse" café racer chassis and a 750-cc Triumph T-120 powerplant, builder Jaye Strait of Britech New England constructed a machine that lives up to Rickmann's reputation as the "Bimota of the 1960s."

Every inch a racer, this bike's components competed in AMA Formula 750 events as far back as 1977. It sports such custom features as Ciriani forks, a 250-millimeter Fontana front brake, and fiberglass fairings, and it currently competes in AHRMA and USCRA-sanctioned "Battle of the Twins" events in the capable hands of racer Greg Nichols. Generating a whopping 76 rear-wheel hp—and a top end of about 150 mph—this nationally competitive race machine has won a Whitworth Cup Championship and recently placed second in an AHRMA event at the Mid-Ohio race course.

1979
AMF/Harley-Davidson FL 1200

The 1200-cc Harley FL of the 1970s was a direct descendant of the late 1940s Hydra-Glide and a cousin of the legendary 1960s Electra-Glide. But the company that produced it had undergone considerable change in the 15 years since the Electra-Glide's debut.

In 1969, Harley-Davidson was bought by the huge American Machine and Foundry Corporation (AMF), which improved management techniques but limited design budgets. The result was a decline in performance and sales throughout the 1970s—despite the

1978
Honda XL 125

When the Beach Boys literally sang the praises of a "little Honda" in a song recorded during their 1960s hey-day, the bike seen here hadn't been built yet—except, perhaps, in spirit. Because even though it hails from the following decade, this is just the kind of motorcycle—small, inexpensive, and fun—that Honda made its early reputation with, and that countless "baby boomers" learned to ride on.

This 1978 XL 125 looks puny when compared to the big bikes that Honda had been making for nearly a decade, but it has a lot of spirit. Although it looks like a trail bike at first glance, it was actually a game little machine that was street-legal, but could also be ridden off-road. It draws its limited power from a 125-cc single-cylinder engine. Unlike the "little Hondas" of the 1960s, however, the XL 125 sports such "modern" features as a tubular steel frame and telescopic front forks. The perfect starter bike, it's likely to stir up happy memories for a generation of first-time riders.

efforts of talented styling chief William ("Willie G.") Davidson, grandson of co-founder Arthur, to develop quality bikes like the 1979 FL 1200 seen here. Harley's slide continued until 1981, when management raised the money to buy the company back from AMF and made the business successful again in the mid-eighties.

This beautifully maintained bike is completely stock except for the chromed engine. Although minus trunk and fairing, it features options like an Andrews cam, dual exhaust, oil cool-er, and auxiliary oil filter. Ridden hard and proud, its original paint is still intact after 75,000 miles of wear!

1980-1989

Looking more like jet planes than motorcycles, high-performance machines employ high technology and new, lightweight materials to go faster than ever before. And while superbike racing becomes an exciting new motor sport, cycle makers strive to put advanced technology into the hands of the everyday rider.

1980 Honda Turbo CBX Custom

Described by its owner as a "monster bike," this heavily customized motorcycle began life as a 1980 Supersport CBX, a model introduced by Honda in 1978. Ohioan Rich Gerhold started from a U.S.-built CBX with a twin-cam 1047-cc motor, then "went to town" rebuilding the bike from the ground up with a ton of custom modifications. He added Suzuki front and rear ends from a 1995 and a 1990 GSXR 1100, with six-piston front brakes and progressive shocks on the back. More additions included a customized frame and seat, a gold drive chain, anodized fittings, stainless-steel oil lines, and a chrome Suzuki headlamp. And the engine itself has been extensively modified with a 67-millimeter bore kit, flat-top turbine pistons, Carillo rods, an F-40 turbocharger, and more.

What all this means is that the CBX is now essentially a showbike, since its 400-plus horsepower makes it, by

Rich's own admission, "spooky to ride." It has reached 140 mph in a sprint, but the lift generated at top speed could cause it to actually take flight! So it remains earthbound, a remarkable example of motorcycle customization.

1981
Yamaha XS1100G

The tuning-fork logo appearing on early Yamaha motorcycles refers to the Japanese cycle maker's parent company, Nippon Gakki, among the world's leading manufacturers of musical instruments. The first Yamaha (named after Nippon Gakki's founder, Torakusu Yamaha) was a two-stroke single, the 125-cc YA-1, introduced in 1955; a series of twin machines appeared in 1957. And just over two decades later, in 1978, the marque launched its first attempt at a four-cylinder superbike—the XS1100.

With a muscular air-cooled 1101-cc twin-cam engine, the shaft-driven XS1100 had plenty of power and a top speed of 135 mph. Its bulky frame, however, was barely strong enough to support its massive powerplant, and as a result there were considerable handling and stability problems at high speeds. But its otherwise smooth ride made the bike, represented here by an all-original 1980 XS1100G, a good choice for towing a sidecar like this Ural rig.

1982
Yamaha Vision

Witness the Yamaha Vision: a motorcycle in many ways ahead of its time, yet also in the wrong place at the wrong time. Introduced in 1982, the 550-cc Vision met with critical acclaim for its performance and its looks. It featured a powerful aluminum V-twin engine with liquid-cooling for tighter tolerances, and a shaft drive and comfortable seating that made long, uninterrupted rides enjoyable.

Extremely agile for its time, the Vision handled well, transitioned smoothly, and, unlike many bikes, didn't require a downshift to pass comfortably. It was easy to ride and maintain, and many riders speak fondly of the Vision as a great first bike. And its sleek, "café racer" styling was timeless, as this handsome black 1982 specimen illustrates.

So why was it discontinued after two years? Well, 1982 also saw the introduction of the Honda Interceptor and the Kawasaki GPZ—two successfully marketed "café racers" that left the Vision in the dust.

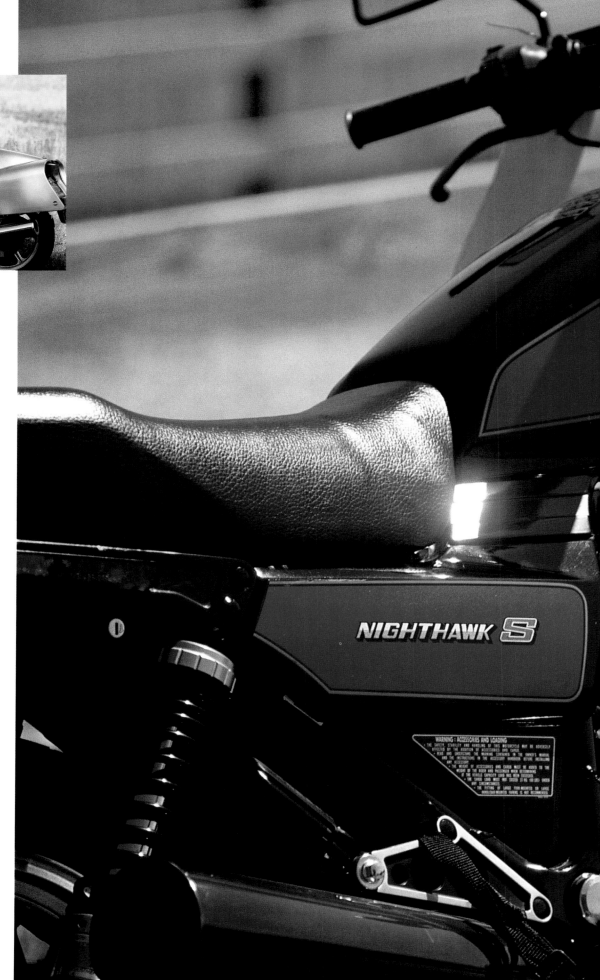

1983
Laverda RGS 1000
Executive

Judging from its high-tech, sculptural, built-for-speed styling, one might expect the sophisticated Laverda Executive to deliver a superfast ride as smooth as the contours of its elegant bodywork. But looks can be deceiving.

With its monstrous three-cylinder 981-cc engine, the RGS 1000, shown here in a 1983 configuration, delivered the goods as far as power was concerned. The tuned version of this machine—the renowned Jota superbike—was the world's fastest production motorcycle of the late 1970s, with a top speed approaching 140 mph. The Italian firm of Laverda, which achieved initial success with agricultural equipment, never had a problem producing powerful machinery.

No, lack of power was not the Executive's problem... but lack of handling often could be. Its futuristic design belied the fact that the RGS 1000 tended to become unstable at high speeds and was prone to shaking violently. But this hitch didn't stop it from cutting an impressive figure throughout the 1980s, and the Executive remains a compelling example of the powerful motorcycles on which Laverda built a worldwide reputation.

1984 Honda Nighthawk 700S

Judging from what owners have to say about it, the Honda Nighthawk S is a motorcycle built to *ride*. The original 1984 machine displayed here is a 700-cc model, which was not subject to the tariff levied on bikes over 700 cc imported to the United States. Consequently, at a sticker price of about $3,400 new, it was considerably less expensive than the VFR750 sportbike, and therefore a bit more accessible to buyers.

People who ride the Nighthawk S just can't say enough about it. A true "all-day rider," this six-speed bike starts at the touch of a button, holds two people and luggage easily, and doesn't tire its rider out. Its features include front double-disk and rear drum brakes; the second generation of Honda's track-suspension system, with adjustable rear forks and hydraulic lifters that never need adjustment; and a dash-panel gear-position indicator.

Easy to maintain and a joy to ride, this Nighthawk S "never sits, except to clean it up every once in a while," according to its rider—who considers himself the "caretaker" rather than the "owner" of this well-preserved original bike.

1985
Honda Z50 SE
Mini Trail

Gleaming from end to end, this little
two-wheeled wonder—a 1985 Honda
Z50 SE Mini Trail—is yet another
example of the Japanese giant's ability
to produce good-quality bikes at both
ends of the size and use spectrum.
The machine is configured for
minibike racing, complete with competition numbers and lots of chrome.
Just right for teaching kids the joys
of two-wheeled travel, this neat little
vehicle provided its owner's children
with a great deal of fun—and will
someday do the same for his grand-
kids. Harkening back to those days
in the early 1950s when nearly all of
Honda's output was this tiny, the Z50
is a pleasant reminder that good things
do come in small packages.

1986
Godden GR500
MK5 Speedway
Racer

Racing motorcycles come in a dizzy-
ing array of frame types, engine cate-
gories, and specializations, depending
on the kind of competition the bike is
intended for. There are road-racers,
dirt-trackers, superbikes, TTs, drag-
sters, motocross, hillclimbers, trials,
enduros, and even sidecar, ice, and
desert racers. But perhaps the most
specialized and unique type is the
speedway bike.

The modern speedway machine,
whose basic design hasn't changed
much in 50 years, is produced specifi-
cally to compete in counterclockwise
four-lap races on oval dirt courses a
quarter-mile long. Powered by
methanol-fueled, four-stroke, 500-cc
singles, these brakeless one-gear
cycles are slid in and out of turns at

high speeds by their riders' maneuver-
ing skills and body weight. In such a
short run, the first bike "out of the box"
will often win the minute-long race.

This hard-ridden 1985 Godden GR500
MK5 displays many unique features
common to speedway racers: small
crossbar-mounted fuel tank; minimal
handlebar controls; steeply angled,
telescopic forks; minimal front suspension; single-cylinder engine; and a
front tire much larger and narrower
than that on the rear.

of superbike design—the company produced the comparatively modest SRX 250 shown here. With a sticker price of around $2,200 new, the 250-cc machine was the smallest of Yamaha's SRX family, which also included the popular SRX 6.

Although it quickly fell out of fashion during the 1980s and was only produced for one year, the SRX 250 has proven itself a dependable, fun-to-ride motorcycle. The owner of this well-kept original says she "just loves it."

1987
Yamaha SRX 250

Diversity has long been a hallmark of Japan's motorcycle industry, perhaps because many Japanese firms competed to fill whatever niche presented itself in the market. Most began with small, inexpensive bikes, then "graduated" to larger machines after years of development, market experience, and fierce competition at home and abroad. Yamaha, the second of Japan's "Big Four," gradually expanded its product lines to include perhaps the widest range of bikes offered by any of the world's cycle makers.

In 1987—the same year in which its remarkable four-cylinder FZR1000 brought Yamaha to the cutting edge

1988
Suzuki 1400
Intruder

Through the 1970s and into the 1980s, Suzuki continued its steady progress as a leading producer of large, powerful, well-designed motorcycles. The striking, shark-like, four-cylinder 997-cc Katana, launched in 1982, featured radical styling by the German firm of Target Design. And another advanced machine on the road in 1988—the Suzuki Intruder—would rank among the earliest and most popular Japanese "cruisers" on the market, surviving well into the 1990s.

Although other versions of the Intruder have appeared over the years, the model's best-known incarnation is the powerful 1400-cc machine represented by the 1995 model shown here. The owner simply calls his bike a "finely built, reliable motorcycle" that he can crank up and ride year after year. Apart from the tank bag, luggage rack, and windshield added by the owner, this Intruder is all stock—and a fine example of modern Japanese motorcycling at its best.

1989
Yamaha VMX 12
Vmax

Launched in the middle of the 1980s, Yamaha's VMX 12 Vmax is definitely a bike with an attitude. The catalog for the Guggenheim Museum's "Art of the Motorcycle" exhibition, in which this 1989 Vmax appeared, describes its appearance as "just a big chunk of engine sitting in a Bronze Age frame."

And a big chunk it is, too—a huge, transverse-mounted, liquid-cooled, 16-valve 1198-cc V-4. But not yet satisfied, Yamaha cranked up the horses to 120 with the "V-Boost" system. As a result, this behemoth can rip through a quarter-mile in ten seconds!

For the most part, Vmax riders have registered their approval of the bike, but with some advice: Don't go cross-country without modifying the seat (it gets a little rough); don't try to beat someone out unless it's on a straight line (you'll regret it); and gentlemen, forget about sitting in the passenger seat— it's just not built for you!

1990
Cotton/Triumph
Racer

Since 1920, the company named for British cycle designer F. Willoughby Cotton has produced bikes known for their superb handling qualities, especially on the race course. The "Cotton" logo, in fact, refers to Stanley Woods' Tourist Trophy victory on a Cotton in 1923. But unlike many marques, Cotton has never used an engine of its own manufacture or design.

Early on, Cotton machines featured Blackburne engines; later, overhead-valve and single motors built by JAP were employed, as were Villiers two-strokes. After World War II, Python, Minarelli, and DMW were among the manufacturers whose engines appeared in Cotton motorcycles.

During the fifties and sixties, Cottons, including the Telstar racer, were again powered by Villiers two-strokes, and the company began producing a new model featuring a Rotax engine in the seventies. In recent years, however, Cotton has supplied kits to motorcyclists who prefer to build their own machines from the frame up. This 1990-era kit-built Cotton racer is just such a bike; its owner fitted the frame with a peppy Triumph single.

1990-2000

As the world approaches a new millennium, the motorcycle gains new-found popularity. Harley-Davidson reinvents its future by looking to the past, creating new markets among riders of all ages. And scores of small cycle makers produce innovative machines to fill every niche, taking two-wheeled technology into the next century and beyond.

1991
"Red Beast"
Composite Custom

It's a car... it's a bike... it's a... beast! Some custom vehicles defy description—and the homemade "Red Beast" is among them. Ohio auto dealer Monroe Young built this incredible machine in the early 1990s with car and motorcycle components.

The Beast's front end, which came from a Kawasaki police bike, has a large-capacity radiator to cool the vehicle while running at parade speed. The machine also sports a 1964 Ford

Falcon rear end and boat-trailer fenders. A 1966 Mustang 289-cubic-inch engine, with 351 heads and a 750 double-pumper carburetor, provides enough horsepower to send the Beast "flying" at 130 mph. Ford claims its engine could reach 180 mph—a speed at which the 1100-pound Beast might literally take off!

Young has fitted the two-seater with stereo, cruise control, cushions, and other features to keep him and his wife Connie comfortable on the road. The couple has traveled much of the country in the Red Beast, turning heads and raising smiles wherever they go. Only too pleased to give disabled children rides, drive in parades, and otherwise generate good will, the Youngs simply love making others happy with this extraordinary machine.

1992
Suzuki 1400
Intruder

To really get to know a particular motorcycle, just listen to what the owner-rider of that model has to say. Who better to tell what that bike you've always wanted really has in store for you—both pro and con?

A rider of a Suzuki 1400 Intruder has called it "one of the most beautiful pieces of rolling stock ever produced; if you want to turn heads, this is your bike." Indeed, the formidable Japanese cruiser is not too shabby where styling is concerned. It sports a lean, sinewy profile; great bodywork that nicely frames the clean lines of the V-twin engine, which in itself is a looker; and an abundance of chrome—features that are evident on the beautiful 1993 Intruder shown here, which hit the market in 1992.

Some Intruder riders remind you that "you're sitting on a whole lotta mule," while others warn about such pitfalls as torque wheelies in first gear, or the "medieval torture device" that passes for a seat. But the one thing they agree on? "Ride one and see for yourself."

1993
Ducati 851
Superbike

The overwhelming image of power suggested by this "big red machine" makes it a bit hard to believe that the first Ducati machines were little engines that clipped onto bicycles. That indeed is where the marque began in 1946, but it has traveled far since then—into the fantastic realm of the superbike.

Screaming out in the vivid red of Italian racing, the Ducati 851 conjures up a vision of breathtaking speed even when it's standing still. Then one grasps the somewhat frightening fact that this is actually a road machine—the most complex ever built by Ducati—although it was the basis for the champion 888 Superbike racer. The heart of this bike, buried within its tubular trellis frame and concealed by sleek body work, is its 851-cc 90-degree V-twin engine. Water-cooled and fuel-injected, this fearsome powerplant employs a double overhead camshaft and eight valves, with Ducati's unique Desmodromic valve operation.

Not exactly a motorcycle for the meek, this 1993 Ducati 851 looks fast, and is. When challenged by a confident rider, it will propel him or her at a cool 160 mph.

1994-1995

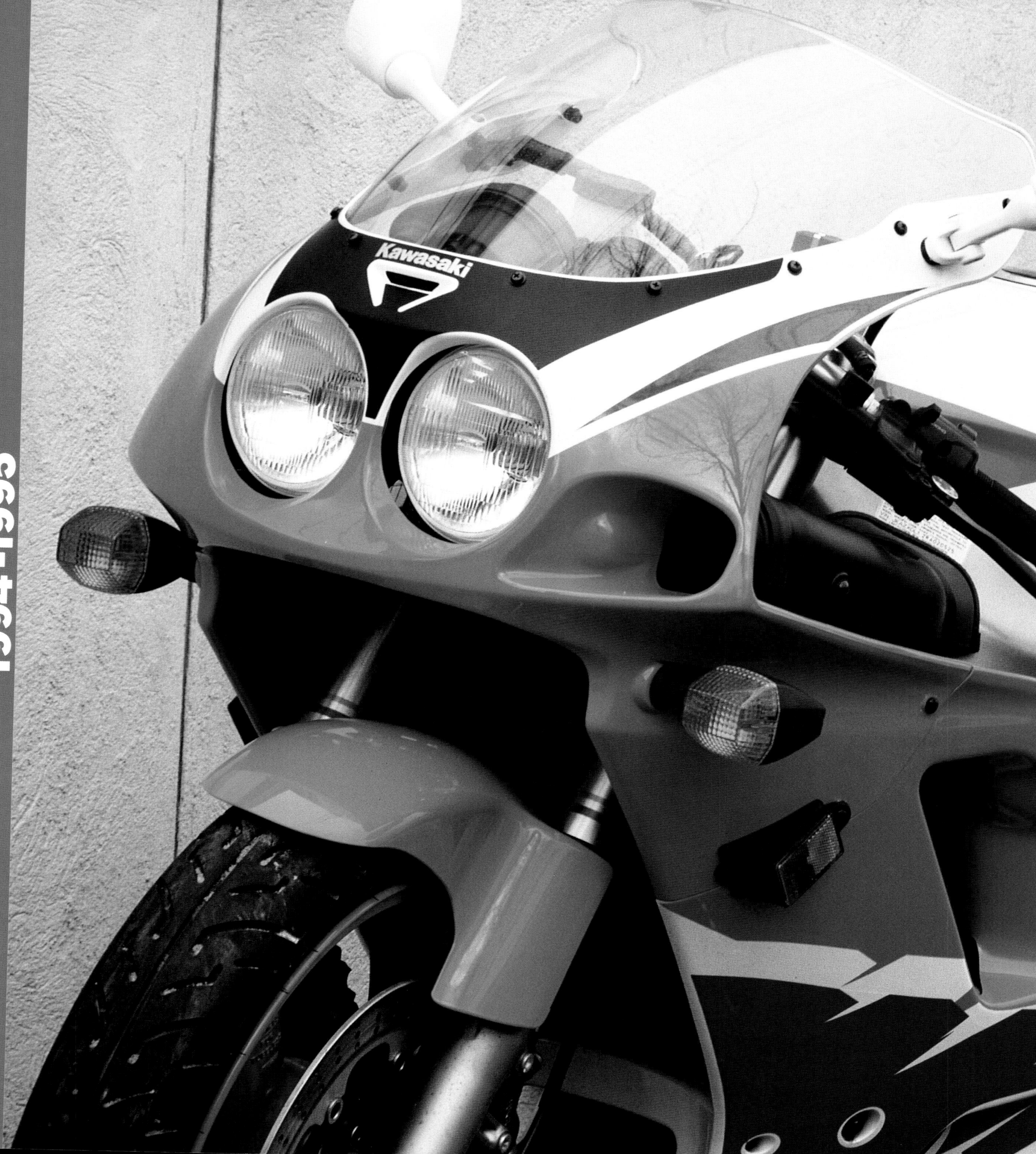

1994
Kawasaki Ninja

Although the smallest of Japan's "Big Four" in motorcycle production, Kawasaki is an industrial giant with interests in many manufacturing fields. And unlike its domestic competitors, the company never "started out small," instead concentrating on producing high-performance machines for riders with a penchant for speed.

Introduced in the 1980s, the Kawasaki Ninja is just such a motorcycle. Named for the mysterious Japanese martial artists/assassins prevalent in contemporary fiction, movies, and video games, this bike is indeed a "killer," in styling as well as performance.

Its low-slung, fully faired, brightly colored body makes this 1994 Ninja look right at home on a video screen or in a comic book. But that toy-like exterior conceals an alloy frame cradling a potent engine capable of unholy speeds approaching 180 mph. One Ninja owner remarked that he could open his machine up to the limit if he wanted to, but simply didn't want to—probably a very good idea!

1995
Honda GL 1500
Gold Wing

The now-legendary Gold Wing represented another big step in Honda's methodical progression from a manufacturer of inexpensive alternative transportation to one of the world's leading producers of sophisticated vehicles of both the two- and four-wheeled variety. At the time of its 1975 launch, the original Honda Gold Wing was a 1000-cc flat-four machine without fairing, windshield, saddlebag, or trunk. As the model caught on with long-distance riders who modified it for touring themselves, Honda responded by equipping later versions with an increasing array of "bells and whistles."

This 20th-anniversary edition of the 1995 GL 1500 Gold Wing shows just how much the model has grown over its two decades of life. Built at Honda's Ohio plant since 1981, the Gold Wing

is now a gargantuan luxury cruiser powered by a water-cooled 1500-cc flat-six. The fully faired, 800-pound bike sports a top rear trunk, side "saddlebags," adjustable windscreen, radio/cassette player, and a host of other features.

Owned by an Ohio couple who has ridden it from coast to coast, this two-toned 1995 "Wing" has traveled some 24,000 miles—and is "still being broken in."

1997 Harley-Davidson Road King

Few decades of this century could pass by without encountering at least one important or influential motorcycle from the American motorcycle company, Harley-Davidson. And no review of the 1990s would be complete without mention of the ultimate American tourer, the Harley-Davidson Road King—two of which are highlighted on the facing page.

A distant relative of Harley's first big twin to feature hydraulic rear brakes and suspension, the 1958 Duo Glide, the Road King is built to travel. This big V-twin machine combines nostalgic styling, touring convenience, and more than enough power to get you there, and it sports such goodies as an oversize headlamp, detachable windshield, studded seat, and hard saddlebags.

The rider of one of the 1997 Road Kings seen here described his ride as "a Barcalounger on wheels"—and he wouldn't have it any other way. When asked why he chose this particular make and model, he replied matter-of-factly, "Because there is only one motorcycle."

1996 Honda GL 1500 Valkyrie

Perhaps worthy of the label, "the Honda for the nineties," the mighty Valkyrie is essentially the same motorcycle as the modern Gold Wing (showcased for 1995), with a few important differences. Both bikes are variants of the same GL 1500 model designation and share the same heart: a liquid-cooled, horizontally opposed six-cylinder engine displacing 1520 cc. And both feature the same electronic ignition, five-speed transmission, brake, and suspension systems.

The major distinction between these two behemoths is essentially one of styling and approach. While the Gold Wing is the ultimate luxury tourer, loaded with creature comforts and virtually fully enclosed, the Valkyrie dispenses with the options and flexes its muscles. When one actually sees that massive six-cylinder engine in all its glory—with its gleaming exhausts thrusting out to the sides—one can't help but be impressed by this mythologically named bike's image of power. The Valkyrie is represented here by a jet-black 1997 model, accompanied by an "electric-lean" California sidecar that pivots diagonally with the bike as it turns.

1998

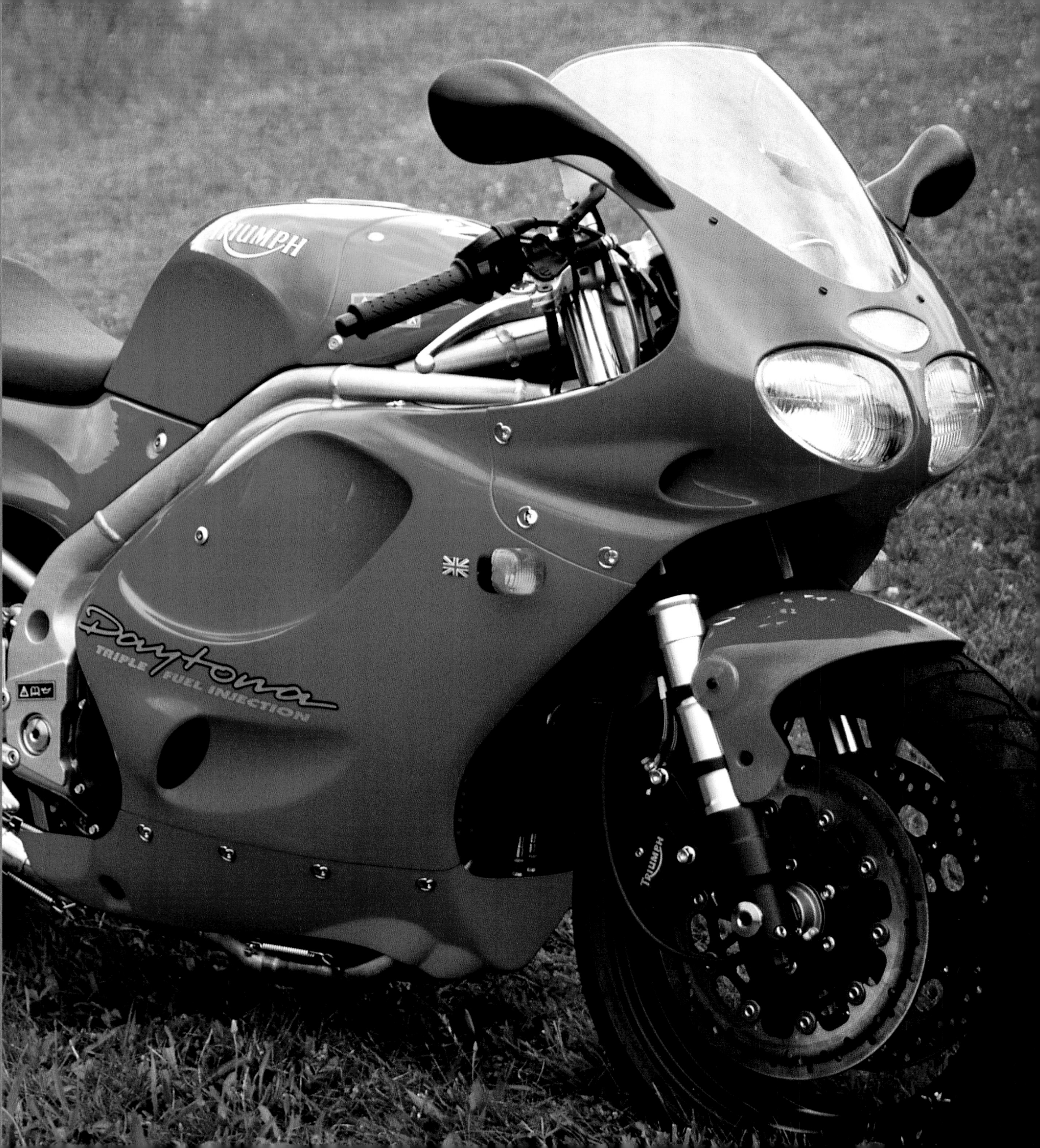

1998 Triumph T595 Daytona

What goes around often does come around, as the saying goes. And in the case of the revered Triumph marque, motorcycling in general is the better for it.

Except for Triumph, there was virtually nothing left of the British motorcycle industry after being knocked senseless by withering competition from Japan and the rest of the world in the 1970s. Then, in 1983, even Triumph itself went into liquidation, and that seemed to be that.

But not to British millionaire John Bloor, who purchased the rights to the marque and secretly developed a new Triumph line in a brand-new factory at Hinckley. In 1991, "the new Triumph" unleashed six new roadsters featuring three- and four-cylinder water-cooled engines, modular design, and lightweight components. With new models like the Daytona, Triumph was off and running again.

The heart of the tornado-red 1998 T595 Daytona shown here is its liquid-cooled, double-overhead-cam, in-line, three-cylinder 955-cc engine, supported by an aluminum-alloy frame, sophisticated suspension and braking, and digital ignition. One wicked-looking machine, this high-performance superbike stands poised to roar into the next century.

1999
BMW R 1200 C

Some things never change… well, almost never. Of course, even the precise, time-honored, traditional BMW way of doing things has to change sometime—but only as much as is absolutely necessary! But the legendary German motorcycle (and auto) producer certainly has kept up with the times—and, as usual, stays on the cutting edge of motorcycle technology. They even offer colors besides the traditional BMW black!

Take the series of startling styling advances BMW began taking back in the 1970s with the smoked-orange R 90 S (with a bikini fairing!) and, in the 1980s and 1990s, with the K1 super-bike, the R 1100 RS sports-tourer, and the stylish F650 single.

Next comes the stunning BMW R 1200 C cruiser, as pictured here in an ivory-colored 1999 version. Powered by an 1170-cc air/oil-cooled twin, the R 1200 features fuel injection, electronic ignition, shaft drive, and antilock brakes.

With considerable power, high torque, superb handling, and extraordinary styling, the R 1200 is a true state-of-the-art motorcycle that will fit as comfortably in the next century as it does in this one.

2000
Buell S1 Lightning

The first year of a new century is a time to look back at what's been achieved over the past 100 years, and forward to the possibilities ahead. Barely a year into the twentieth century, Bill Harley and Arthur Davidson began tinkering with a motorbike in a backyard shed and looked ahead. Before too many decades passed, they had helped create an industry and left a legacy that will live far beyond their own century.

While working for Harley-Davidson in the early 1980s, racing engineer Erik Buell began building his own motorcycles in a barn behind his home, and looked ahead.

Since 1993, the Buell Motorcycle Company has created striking machines with the full backing of Harley-Davidson. Engineered for the twenty-first century, this "spark-red" 1998 S1 Lightning features Harley's 1203-cc Evolution powerplant and Buell's forward-thinking designs. The Thunderbolt S2 and S3 sports-tourers and Cyclone M2 sportbike are among other Buell models. Each employs innovative and sophisticated systems designed to take American motorcycling into the next milennium.

The Next Century

Looking back, it's hard to believe that one of Erik Buell's futuristic sports-tourers is a descendant of Harley-Davidson's "Silent Gray Fellow"—or that the 1998 T595 Daytona has any connection whatsoever with the Triumph Single of 1921.

But the connection, of course, is there. When you take a contemporary sport-bike and strip away its carbon-fiber fairings, electronic components, sophisticated systems, and high-performance parts, you have a machine that still works much like a motorcycle did 100 years ago. The biggest difference is a century's worth of progress in materials production, engine development, styling and systems design, and road and track experience. It may look like a jet plane, but it's still a motorcycle.

Take a gander at other 1990s bikes, however, and you might do a double take—because the machine looks a lot like its "grandfather" from a half-century ago. Much of the styling of today's Road Kings and Valkyries harkens back to the big Indian Chiefs and Harley Glides of the 1950s. Are riders' tastes taking a great leap backward?

Looking ahead, it seems an interesting dichotomy has developed regarding what motorcyclists want to see—and ride—in the coming century. Analysts predict that motorcycling's rising popularity will continue, especially among the 33-to-64 age group. Everyone wants increased performance, handling, and comfort. But to those legions of bikers to whom "motorcycle" means "Harley-Davidson," the ever-more-powerful, customized machines they ride will have to look a good deal like Harleys of the past.

This holds true even if those bikes are actually built by one of many American "micro-manufacturers" that have sprung up to satisfy the demand for big V-twins that Harley-Davidson itself created but can't fill. And ironically, a few larger American companies are gearing up to give Harley

some real competition in the decades to come. These include the reborn Excelsior-Henderson firm, which hopes to begin production of a new Super-X V-twin by the end of 1998, and snowmobile-maker Polaris, which plans to launch its own big V-twin bike, the Victory, before the end of this century.

On the other side of the wheel are the sportbike enthusiasts who flock toward aggressively styled (translation: mean-looking), unbelievably fast superbikes whose "streetfighter" image is a direct throwback to the in-your-face attitude of the café racers of the 1950s and 1960s. These edge-of-the-millenium rebels are cut from the same cloth as the rock 'n' rollers who created a subculture of their own based in such roadside hang-outs as London's Ace Café 40 years ago. The difference between today's superbikers and the "ton-up boys"—named for their quest to achieve the "ton," or 100 mph—is that the latter-day "wild ones" ride machines capable of 150 mph without breaking a sweat.

So the stage is set for a parade of ever-faster machines to roar into the twenty-first century. They'll come from all over the world, from new companies and old. And their new innovations—emerging from diverse design philosophies—will attempt to satisfy an ever-wider variety of riders.

Many will represent new twists on old formulas, as in Harley-Davidson's new Twin-Cam 88 engine, introduced on some 1999 models. It's still an air-cooled, 45-degree, pushrod V-twin, but it's punched out to 1450 cc—more than any Harley engine before it.

Others, like Buell, will continue to modify proven engines while redefining frame construction to reduce weight, maximize rigidity, and centralize mass. Still others will introduce revolutionary engines like Honda's V-4, or Bimota's advanced two-strokes, made viable by a new generation of materials and processes. Whatever happens, the twenty-first century should be at least as interesting—and eventful—as the one that preceded it.

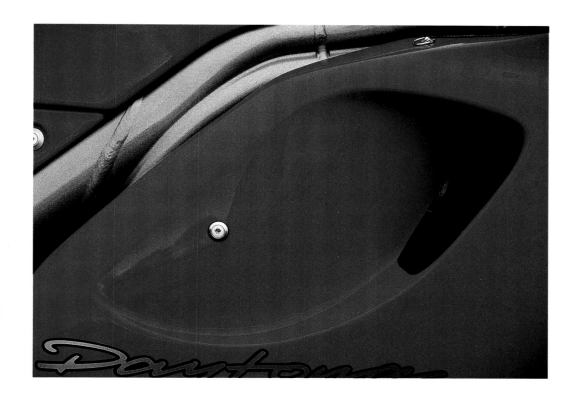

Motorcycle Museums and Collections

The following museums are just a few of many institutions worldwide with significant collections of historic motorcycles, some of which appear in this book:

Allen Vintage Motorcycle Museum
Boston, MA
(By appointment only)
www.allenmuseum.com
Email: ACAllenCo@aol.com

Barber Vintage Motorsports Museum
512 28th Street South
Birmingham, AL 35233
205-252-8377

Harley-Davidson Museum & Factory
Tour Center
Route 30
York, PA
717-848-1177

Indian Motocycle Museum/
Hall of Fame
33 Hendee Street
P.O. Box 90003, Mason Sq. Station
Springfield, MA 01139
413-737-2624
www.sidecar.com/indian

Motorcycle Heritage Museum
33 Collegeview Road
Westerville, OH 43081
614-882-2782

National Motor Museum
John Montagu Building
Beaulieu, Hampshire S042 7ZN, U.K.
Tel: 01590-612-345
www.beaulieu.co.uk/museum
Email: museum@beaulieu.co.uk

National Motorcycle Museum (U.K.)
Coventry Road, Bickenhall
Solihull, W. Midlands, U.K.

National Motorcycle Museum
(Australia)
25 Kemble Court
Mitchell, ACT 2911, Australia
www.ozemail.com.au/~museum

Old Rhinebeck Aerodrome
42 Stone Church Road
Rhinebeck, NY 12572
914-758-8610

Otis Chandler Vintage Museum of
Transportation and Wildlife
1421 Emerson Avenue
Oxnard, CA 93030
805-486-5929

Rocky Mountain Motorcycle Museum
and Hall of Fame
308 E. Arvada Street
Colorado Springs, CO 80906
719-633-6329
www.travelassist.com/mag/a20.html

Sammy Miller Museum
Gore Road
New Milton, Hampshire, U.K.
Tel: 01425-620-777
www.motorcycle.com/mo/mcfrank/
sammymuseum

Trev Deeley Motorcycle Museum
13500 Verdun Place
Richmond, British Columbia
Canada
604-273-5421
www.canadianbiker.com/deeley1.html

Internet "Virtual" Motorcycle Museums (online only)

Motorcycle Museum Online
www2.tower.org/museum/main/html

Motorcycle Web Museum
www.tedoc.nl/WebCycles

Motorcycling Organizations

At the right is a listing of some significant organizations providing support, information, and programs for motorcycle owners, riders, and enthusiasts in the United States and abroad.

American Historic Racing Motorcycle
Association (AHRMA)
P.O. Box 882
Wausau, WI 54402-0882
715-842-9699
www.ahrma.org

American Motorcyclist Association
(AMA)
33 Collegeview Road
Westerville, OH 43081-1484
614-891-2425
Membership Info: 1-800-AMA-JOIN

Antique Motorcycle Club of America
2411 Middle Road
Davenport, IA 52803
319-324-8137

Motorcycle Owners & Riders
Association (MORA)
P.O. Box 707
Gresham, OR 97030
503-665-6301

Motorcycle Industry Council, Inc.
2 Jenner Street/Suite 150
Irvine, CA 92718
Motorcycle Rider Course Info: 1-800-447-4700

National Coalition of Motorcyclists
15910 Ventura Blvd./Suite 1712
Encino, CA 91436
1-800-235-2424 (in CA)
1-800-525-5355 (outside CA)

National Organization for
Responsible Motorcycling (NORM)
Box 1594
Rockville, MD 20849
703-556-7392

Vintage Motorcycle Enthusiasts
7521 126th Avenue N.E.
Kirkland, WA 98033

Women on Wheels((WOW)
P.O. Box 26
Fall River, WI 53932
1-800-322-1969
www.visi.com/~stacy/WOW.html

Photo Credits

Copyright Solomon R. Guggenheim Foundation, New York, Photographer David Heald: Page 12 (1901 Thomas, collection of William Eggers); Page 19 (1908 FN Four, collection of Chris Le Sauvage); Page 80 (1945 Harley-Davidson Model U, U.S. Navy, collection of Chris Le Sauvage)

Copyright National Motor Museum, Beaulieu, U.K.: Page 13 (1902 Werner); Page 15 (1904 Phoenix): Page 16 (1905 Matchless Single); Page 17 (1906 NSU); Page 18 (1907 Deronziere); Page 34 (1918 Tusroke); Page 35 (1919 Wooler); Page 52 (1931 Matchless Silver Hawk)

Copyright Jeff Hackett: Page 14 (1903 Clement); Page 22 (1910 Wagner)

Copyright 1999 Marc Bondarenko: Page 47 (1929 Scott Squirrel Sprint Special, collection of Barber Vintage Motorsports Museum, Birmingham, AL); Page 147 (1989 Yamaha VMX 12 Vmax, collection of Barber Vintage Motorsports Museum, Birmingham, AL)

Acknowledgments

The authors would like to thank the many people who made this book possible. First and foremost, to the individual motorcycle owners and enthusiasts who enabled us to photograph their beloved bikes and/or supplied us with invaluable information and advice, we give a hearty "thumbs up":

Fred Anderson, Dale Andrizzi, Dave Axelrod, Tim Bailey, Doc Batsleer, Bob Beards, Garrett Bekker II, Garrett Bekker III, Gregory Bidou, Stephen Bochter, Tom Bowers, Brian and Beth Brooks, Kim Bush, Bob Butler, Keith Campbell, Kyle Campbell, David Carr, Ken Cassens, Ian Chard, Daniel Coyle, Sal Defer, Tim DiBiasi, Robert Doll, George Dragone, Bill Eggers, Aaron Fitch, Thomas Fleming, Randy Forgue, Bill France, Ken Ganz, Rich Gerhold, Ultan Guilfoyl, Jeff Hackett, Richard Haley, Mike Hardin, Jim Hare, Deb Harmon, John Hasty, Frank Haverkamp, Brent Hensley, Jonathan Hughes, Greg Jelkin, Ken Johnson, Don Jones, Dan Kelley, Daniel Kean, Kevin Kirsh, Al Knapp, Robert Lardinais, Chuck Le Cain, Chris Le Sauvage, Buck Lewis, Dale Malasek, Dave Marino, Reed Martin, Paul Mayer, John McCarter, Bob McFettridge, Bob McKenzie, Scott McKenzie, Tom Mickle, Dave Milstein, Don W. Miller, Sam Miller, Murray Moody, Ed Nelson, Geno Palma, Gordon Pittsley, Jeff Ray, Mark Rinehart, Vanessa Rocca, Bob Rourke, David Sarafan, John Schrein, Ken Sitterley, Dave Smith, Jaye Strait, Bob Tater, Roger Terry, Terry Thompson, Ted Tine, Robert B. Totten, Bert Von Wermb, Bob Ward, Robert H. Whitney, Bruce Williams, Heather Williams, Tom Wood, Doug Wothke, Monroe and Connie Young, Art Zamsky, Randy Zussman

Our gratitude also goes to the staffs of the following museums for their kind assistance:

The Barber Vintage Motorsports Museum, Birmingham, AL; The National Motor Museum at Beaulieu, Hampshire, U.K.; Old Rhinebeck Aerodrome Museum, Rhinebeck, NY; The Solomon R. Guggenheim Museum, New York, NY

And a thank you to the members of the following organizations who helped us along the way:

American Historic Racing Motorcycle Association, Wausau, WI; American Motorcyclist Association, Westerville, OH; Antique Motorcycle Club of America, Davenport, IA; Classic Weekend Triumph Days, Sturbridge, MA

Finally, we thank Leslie Daley, who worked so tirelessly on finalizing the layouts; Marilyn Bliss, who prepared the Index with dispatch and professionalism; and Sally Anderson, who copy-edited, proofread, and oversaw the final stages of the project with skill and diplomacy.

A home-built three-wheel motorcycle seen on the streets of Paris in the summer of 1998.

Index